The Ashes That Still Remain

Rev. Thomas R. Koys

The Ashes That Still Remain
By: Reverend Thomas R Koys

ISBN#1-891280-43-0

Publisher:
CMJ Marian Publishers
Post Office Box 661
Oak Lawn, Illinois 60454
www.cmjbooks.com"
jwby@aol.com

Manufactured in the United States of America

Graphic Design: Lisa Duffy
Contact Publisher for information

Editorial Assistant: Cynthia Nicolosi

Lincoln's Right To Life Address
(Drawn by analogy from his actual addresses)

My Fellow Americans!

I am deeply grateful for the opportunity to be with you at this time. I have lived now since 1865 in the Beautiful Life, but I have always followed with the keenest interest the fortunes of my countrymen.

Our greatest happiness here is the vision of the All Holy, but in that vision we also see the people and places most familiar to us on earth. In this way I have followed your vicissitudes from that Good Friday evening in Ford's theater until this moment.

It seems to me that there are times of agony in every generation: in mine, the great agony over the inalienable right to liberty; in yours, the far greater agony over the inalienable right to life. We deplored a bloody war of brother against brother. You deplore a bloodier war against unborn children. During our war, everyone on both sides triggered under the list of casualties after every battle. At the end, well over a million men lay in their graves. But now, in your incredible war against the preborn, you kill more than three times as many innocents in one year as we did in four.

I remember only too well the debates we had before and during the war. There were so many false arguments on both sides. Judge Douglas had a great number of them, as many of you do now. Much debate revolved around the Dred Scott Decision of 1857. Seven to two, the Supreme Court had voted that Negroes are not persons.

So now you debate the Roe Decision of 1973, in which, again by seven to two, the Supreme Court has voted that the preborn are not persons. By these laws, you can do with Negroes and the preborn whatever you please. But unjust laws are no laws at all. As Supreme Court Justice Byron White has so well said, they are but exercises in "raw judicial power."

If not to raw and blind judicial power, then wither must we

turn for justice in the cause of both the Negro and the preborn? I believe we must turn to the sheet anchor of our way to life, the Declaration of Independence. There we find a God given and inalienable right to liberty for the Negro, and a God-given and inalienable right to life for the preborn.

I used to argue that the heart of the matter was whether the Negro was a man. For if he was, the American proposition is that all men are created equal, and so the Negro must be free. But science now shows beyond any honest doubt that a new human being begins life at conception, and, being equal to all others, has an equal right to life. This remains true regardless of gender or race or genetic defect, the age or marital status or career of the mother, or the cruel violence or gross immorality of the father.

So it is also when the preborn become the newborn, or the aged or infirm. They are endowed by their Creator with certain inalienable rights. Among these is the sacred right to life. From this flows our profound conviction, as a people, of the sanctity of human life, from the moment of conception until the moment of natural death. If America is to endure, we must dedicate ourselves again to the realization of this conviction in private and public life, in all our institutions and in all our laws.

But I have now already spoken longer than I did at Gettysburg. Perhaps the reason is that my agony for my country is even greater now than it was then. For our war was waged in the open to the thunder of cannonades, and the corpses lay rotting in the sun until we could bury them. But your slaughter is silent and invisible, and in numbers is immensely greater, and the corpses lie we know not where.

My fellow Americans, I am loathe to close. I can only implore the All Holy to grant you wisdom, and to have mercy upon us all.

"Abraham Lincoln"

Contents

Forward

We live in a pluralistic society. In fact, life would be pretty boring if we were all the same. Yet the word "pluralistic" is an adjective that modifies a singular noun, "society". We live in a society. For it to be one society, something has to hold it together. In the midst of our very legitimate diversity, there has to be something that unites us and some common principles which everyone acknowledges. Indeed, there must be something worth fighting for and even dying for. Otherwise, there is not a pluralistic society, but rather chaos.

Using his knowledge of the Civil War and his love of the Catholic Faith, Fr. Tom Koys draws lessons from both to give his readers a deeper understanding of the pro-life movement. He also motivates them to join that movement, free from the unwarranted fear that to defend the unborn means to oppose what is truly "American" and "mainstream.". The pursuit of justice for the unborn demands virtue and it demands a sense of history. Fr. Koys presents insights into both. His book helps us understand what our Holy Father often says, namely, that freedom must never be divorced from truth.

This book also reminds me of the warning of the Prophet Jeremiah against the false prophets who preach "Peace, Peace: when there is no peace." (see Jer. 6:14) Peace is lost long before guns are fired; peace is lost as soon as a single human being's rights are trampled and equal dignity is denied. To seek peace by ignoring injustice, or by holding that "all opinions are the same", is to abandon the very basis of peace. May America avoid that tragic mistake, and find the courage once again to secure liberty and justice, not just for some but for all. I highly encourage you to read carefully the message of this intriguing book.

Fr. Frank Pavone
National Director, Priests for Life

Introduction

The American Civil War is perhaps the most studied event in the history of modern times. Nearly a century and a half after Fort Sumter received the first round of Confederate fire, the interest of scholars, artists and audiences continues unabated. Well-tended memorials pay homage to men on both sides of the conflict, while Civil War clubs reenact famous battles with meticulous attention to the details of uniform and arms. Just a few years ago, historical film makers Ric and Ken Burns enjoyed an unparalleled success with their multi-part telling of the Civil War story using photos of the time dramatically highlighted by the words of those who experienced the war first hand. The Civil War has also marched in step with the internet as the great number of websites devoted to the subject proves.[1]

Yet, with all this, the passing of time and a shift in cultural values has gradually removed the heart from the Civil War story. Having traded the forest for the trees, we have become experts on the details while missing the point entirely. We have learned to look at the Civil War through the filtering lens of a value-free philosophy with the result that the victory that saved our Union has lost its soul in the re-telling. The quiet but destructive nature of this omission has acted upon our national unity like termites under the White House ballroom. On the surface, everything seems to be moving along nicely, but collapse is inevitable.

I found a graphic illustration of this value-free way of looking at this value-charged war while visiting the beautiful Stone Mountain theme park outside Atlanta, Georgia. Here, on the side of the incredible granite wall, stands the magnificent carving of Confederate President Jackson Davis and Confederate Generals Lee and Jackson. Standing before these images, I had an incredible sense of the goodness of the American people. After all, here I was

---

1. At the time of writing, one search agent yielded 450,208 websites devoted to the Civil War.

in the Deep South, in the shadow of a monument to men who had wished to undo the United States and establish a separate country, and to that end had engaged the Union in a lengthy and bloody war. How could such a memorial exist? But, such is the American character: always looking to make of the vanquished a friend and an equal again. My heart swelled as I recalled Lincoln's last wish to show malice toward none and charity for all. Here, certainly, was the proof that all was forgiven.

Yet, these thoughts of mine took another turn as I entered the park's gift shop and read the words on a T-shirt for sale there. I realized another interpretation was possible. The message on the T-shirt read (I paraphrase):

Once upon a time,
When America was just growing up,
There was an argument among Americans.
A lot of people in the north disagreed with
A lot of people in the south.
A lot of people got hurt.
We pay tribute to the brave and courageous
Who fought on both sides.

The value-free wording of this souvenir of a glorious past was clearly an attempt to describe the Civil War to young school children in a way that would keep little Northern school children from self-righteousness and little Southern school children from embarrassment. As an educational tool, however, it failed miserably to help students of both regions understand anything at all about the Civil War. Indeed, for those who wish to espouse a radical, value-free outlook, the words on this T-shirt could describe any and all conflicts in world history. There are no good guys and no bad guys, no right and wrong — just different points of view.

That may be all right for T-shirt wisdom. The tragedy is that this way of thinking has been the dominant philosophy in our schools, both Northern and Southern, for too long with the result that the vital, nation-defining lessons of the Civil War have been lost. Future generations are being deprived of a patrimony of principle and heroism upon which they could build a just and prosperous society.

I can remember from my grade school years, when I first heard there was such a thing as an American Civil War, the importance my teachers put on understanding "the causes of the war." Every test had such a question, and every teacher tried to make it into a memorable classroom discussion. Even then, as a student, I suspected something very different in our treatment of the American Civil War from our study of other wars. In just about every other case there was general agreement about the reason why a war had happened. Even given a selection of mitigating circumstances, a *cause célèbre* would emerge by which a war could be understood and its lessons derived. For example, the American Revolution took place to win independence from England in the name of our right to self-govern. World War II stopped the Nazis from taking over the world. Even the Vietnam War, although the value of the fight was certainly hotly debated, was motivated by the desire to put a halt to communism in the Far East and encourage the spread of democracy.

A consensus of opinion on the cause of the Civil War, however, always remained lacking. What is worse, some very notable scholars have held the position that no final judgement can be made. Consider this excerpt from the introduction to Kenneth M. Stampp's *The Causes of the Civil War*.

As one reflects upon the problem of causation one is driven to the conclusion that historians will never know, objectively and with mathematical precision, what caused the Civil War. Working with fragmentary evidence, possessing less than a perfect understanding of human behavior, viewing the past from the perspective of their own times, finding it impossible to isolate one historical event to test its significance apart from all others, historians must necessarily be somewhat tentative and conjectural in offering their interpretations.[2]

What is it about the Civil War that makes schoolteachers, historians, politicians and ordinary people of all kinds so argumentative about its cause? Why is it that the most visited chat rooms on Civil War websites are those that deal with its cause?

The answer lies in a psychological or, if you will, spiritual fact: it is always hardest to look at oneself objectively. We would have no difficulty evaluating 20th century Germany, for example, where I am sure the debate continues about why and how the Nazis came to power. The German people can be divided into three groups: those who can say neither they nor their family ever supported the Nazis in the first place; those who must admit that they or their near relatives supported the Nazis and have since had a great political conversion; and finally, those who are still toying with the idea that the Nazis had it right. Much to the credit of Germans today, most individuals fall into the first and second categories with only a minority representing group three. There is general agreement among Germans about who the "bad guys" were, even if some of them happened to be relatives.

I mention all this simply as a backdrop to our discussion of the Civil War. What may seem so clear to us about the political history of another people does not emerge so easily when we give an eye to our own story.

In each of the wars I mentioned above there is an easily identifiable "us" versus "them" scenario. But in the American Civil War, we hold back from making such clear distinctions. You might

---

2. Kenneth M. Stampp, *The Causes of the Civil War* (New York, NY: Simon & Schuster, Inc., 1986), p. 5

ask, isn't it an easy split? South and North? Not so. The antagonists of the Civil War were not defined simply by geography. If that were the case, there would be no hesitation in naming the cause of the war. The problem is that the Civil War hung on a question not of locality but of principle. The South wanted to continue to hold men as slaves and did not want the North telling them they couldn't. It might have been dressed up in the language of state and property rights, but at the bottom of the well was the murky water of an intolerable injustice.

The constant hesitancy to assign "the" cause to the Civil War, with its concomitant reluctance to designate "the enemy," is a sign that common principles of right and wrong are lacking in the soul of our country. To designate the cause and the enemy in the Civil War story, Americans would have to admit that other Americans were not just wrong, but terribly wrong. They would have to admit that a moral evil did, at one time, threaten the continued existence of this nation. They would have to admit that heroes are not defined solely by romantic gestures and the ultimate sacrifice, but by the nature of the cause for which they give their all. This would require not only a ruthless self-honesty, but the admission that moral imperatives do exist, can be recognized, and do sometimes demand a contest.

To what extent have we succumbed to the value-free interpretation of the Civil War? Let us put ourselves to the test: Are we glad the North won? Many Americans would say, "Well, of course! The Union was saved and the slaves were freed." True enough. But let's push the matter further and ask, "Who was it that threatened the Union in the first place?" One can sense almost immediately a shuffling of feet and a hesitation. The mind casts about for an "enemy" but recoils at the suggestion that the enemy were very ordinary Americans, much like ourselves, who failed to see the moral dilemma of slavery, or saw it and chose to look the other way for whatever reason. We have been so well trained to resist being "judgmental" that we can no longer assign praise or blame without feeling at the same time apologetic. But, let us ask ourselves: How can we be enthusiastic about the Union victory without making reference to the errors held by our Southern brothers and sisters? On the other hand, how can we maintain a neutral sentiment about the Civil War without appearing to be racists?

A kind of intellectual seesaw is at work in the American mind over the significance of the Civil War. The need for value-free history has corrupted the whole story and reduced it to a collection of interesting anecdotes and romantic figures. To be interested in the battles, the death counts, the weapons and the strategies solely for their own sake, and to pass this kind of study onto each successive generation as if it were real history, is a tragedy nearly as great as the war itself.

Even as I write this, I can almost hear voices saying, "Why does there have to be *one* cause? Can't it just be that there were several causes and leave it at that?" But if we opt for such a position, if we choose not to pursue the answer to the question "why?" which hovers over the graves of 600,000 fallen Confederate and Union soldiers, we must be prepared to accept the consequences.

There is nothing more divisive in a community than the existence of opposing moral philosophies. Every parent knows the devastating effects to family harmony when mom and dad send out mixed signals about right and wrong. Allowing Johnny to beat up on Joey, but punishing Joey for beating up on Johnny in return always increases the conflict between Joey and Johnny. Call it double standards, unfair, or even "that's life," maintaining two opposing moral philosophies in one community is clearly destructive of peace and happiness. Mom and dad must unite in common agreement about a moral principle that both boys can acknowledge and abide by. The result will be personal security and harmony on the home front.

The real enemy that threatened this nation in the time of the Civil War was just this kind of moral ambiguity. From the very beginning, the Founding Fathers realized that the institution of slavery was by nature opposed to the principles upon which the country was founded and would one day have to be eliminated. Their insight was borne out by historical events as the tension between justice and practice gradually escalated. In the years leading up to the Civil War, African-Americans were defined and redefined by the nation's courts and legislative bodies as less than human. It had to be so, or the public conscience could not have borne the hypocrisy of living in the home of the free while at the same time holding some men and women in chains. Clearly, the laws of the nation failed, even to the highest level of appeal — the United States Supreme Court.

The greatness of this country is owed to the fact that moral ambiguity did not prevail despite years of rhetorical gaming and the force of arms. The South repeatedly rejected the idea that slavery was at the heart of its conflict with the North, or that they had taken up arms to protect the "right" of a white man to own a black man. A cleverly contrived vocabulary avoided the moral question entirely and lowered the argument to the level of state sovereignty or the mere protection of property rights. As much as Lincoln himself wanted to agree with this reasoning, that slavery was not the main issue, he eventually realized it was and the prediction he had once made in his "A House Divided" speech came to pass by his own action in the Emancipation Proclamation. It was as much Lincoln's own conversion on this matter as anything else that saved our nation.

The essence of the Civil War was a clarification and defense of the dignity of the human being. Its cause, therefore, cannot be found within the context of historical facts and details — the temporal phenomena, if you will — but in the eternal and universal truths that act as a light on human history and by which the actions of a people can be judged. Regardless of long-standing cultural practices, economic need, or even the dictates of human courts, the value of the human person remains the fundamental value upon which justice in a society will be defined.

We have here, at the very beginning of our study, the crucible upon which our reflection will turn: the distinction between a universal, transcendent principle and its translation in legal systems. When a harmony exists between these two orders, a society can rightly consider itself just. Laws cannot determine the morality of a people, but they do express the fundamental values towards which a society tends. Even though racism may exist in many American hearts, slavery as an institution does not exist in our laws. The laws are not racist. They stand, therefore, as good guidelines we must strive harder to obey. The non-racist spirit of American law in this sense acts in a teaching manner. Today, the instruction inherent in American political wisdom teaches us to see a brother or sister not only in African-American citizens, but in Indian, Oriental, Muslim, and Mexican as well.

If the fundamental lesson of the Civil War consists in the definition and defense of the human person, then another lesson emerges almost directly as a result of the first: law serves justice, it does not define it. The philosophical light necessary to answer the question, "Is the black man a person?" would lead to the answer to the following question, "Is the black man a person under the law?" If so, then he merits the full protection of the law and any attack upon his freedom is an attack upon the fundamental human rights enjoyed by all citizens. He falls under the protection of beliefs espoused in the Declaration of Independence, the Bill of Rights, and the Constitution. To defend those rights, wars may be fought.

Turning now to our own time, we find the same fundamental question being posed again, this time of the unborn child. Is the unborn child a person? If so, than he merits the full protection of the law. Sadly, history is repeating itself. Despite the overwhelming evidence of science and the contributions of psychology and philosophy, the unborn child remains less than human in the eyes of those who make and interpret our laws.

As a result, within the national consciousness there lies once again a twisting and turning pangs of self-accusation even worse than in the years preceding the Civil War. Today there is no Underground Railroad for the helpless innocence at rest in the womb. Stripped of all legal protection, the unborn child has no voice but the conscience of his mother who, more often than not, is as much a victim as the child she will give up to death.

The abortion issue, so often presented as a private matter for the expectant mother alone to decide, actually involves and implicates the entire nation because the future of the American ideal lies at stake once again. If any human being within the jurisdiction of these United States fails to receive the full protection of her laws, then America faces eventual and certain decay. America is what she is because of her commitment to human freedom, as every immigrant who came into New York Harbor under Liberty's triumphant torch knows. The slight of hand which makes "freedom" the right of a woman to abortion without reference to the unborn human life within her has its historical roots in the rhetoric of Southern slave owners who spoke passionately in defense of their property rights without acknowledging that the property in question was a human being. Really, when it comes to the arguments for legalized abortion, even the amateur historian would conclude America has "been there, done that."

On the philosophical level, though the South lost the war, it is not difficult to conclude that it won the battle for the American mind. Philosophically speaking, it is Jefferson Davis, not Abraham Lincoln, who embodies our spirit as we cross into the 21st century. The willingness, even eagerness, to live with moral ambiguity and to covet peace at the expense of truth and justice, to preserve entrenched institutions and the status quo and to complacently accept what the previous generation has passed along as its legacy of "a just society" — these were the spoils of war left to us a century after Lee surrendered at Appomattox.

One of the great marks of contemporary society, about which politicians, business executives, educators and clergy speak unceasingly, is the notion of "community." But how such a vast community as ours can sustain unity while simultaneously trying to prevent the emergence of a common moral philosophy is a riddle yet to be solved.

It is true that the century's bitter experience with radical ideologies has left the world wary of absolute truths. To protect itself against further harm, society has chosen instead a path not only of *ethnic* diversity but *ethical* diversity. In the name of peace, people agree to tolerate ethical systems different than their own as if ethics were a kind of grocery market of values: we like Wheaties and they like Cornflakes. The great popularity of New Age religion, derived as it is from eastern sources, can be understood as a desire to replace absolutes with an unrestrained relativism in which anything goes. That way, so we like to think, nobody will get hurt.

Yet, such a system, while understandable in the historical context of a violent century, cannot produce true and lasting peace. On the contrary, the presence of different systems of morality in a single society is a sure path to societal chaos. This is not to condemn cultural diversity. Our present appreciation of cultural pluralism is a great blessing which can only solidify our unity as a nation and a world community. But if by cultural pluralism we mean abdicating the seat of judgement over what is just and unjust in human affairs, that which promises us peace will inevitably recoil on itself with violence. Legalized abortion is the proof of this claim.

The watering-down of the fundamental lessons of the Civil War is nowhere more apparent than in the American Africans* community's silence on the abortion issue. One would expect African-Americans to be the most vocal in defense of life, recognizing in the unborn their forebears in chains, without representation or rights before the law. Oddly enough, it would

---

* I use this term intentionally to promote a more unique American culture.

seem as though American Africans had themselves forgotten the cornerstone of their own liberation. The Civil Rights movement is given ample space in literature and documentary, but it too, like the Civil War, has fallen more and more under the influence of value-free thinking. As a consequence, the foundation of civil rights — the dignity and worth of the individual human being — has been lost. In lieu of the fundamental rights of the human person, racial conflicts today are supposed to be resolved under the banner of "cultural diversity." But such apparently noble jargon nimbly side steps the central issue of personhood and inevitably leaves conflicts unresolved.

The reluctance to call a spade a spade in the Civil War story harkens back to the "peace at all cost" reasoning of that period's politicians as they scrambled with last minute compromises to forestall war. There are many today who would say, "So what if the North American continent had been divided into two or more countries? Isn't that better than even one person killed in action?"

While most of us prefer the language of peace over the prospect of conflict, the love of peace does not exclude engagement in war. We have only to consider the heroic examples of Mother Teresa of Calcutta or John Paul II to realize it is possible to be a pacifist and a fighter at the same time. These are not weak, morally indecisive people. They have been outspoken in their defense of justice and they have borne the criticism and active opposition of many of their contemporaries. They teach us that peace is not merely the absence of arms, but a clear and decisive commitment to what is right. Peace without justice is a dangerous illusion.

Returning now to the Civil War, how can we bask in the triumph over slavery and the strength of our national unity while at the same time condemning the fighting spirit that won the day? Why should we be ashamed at the victory that brought about such great good for so many? Do we fully appreciate the contributions of American Africans who gradually and steadily rose from the shadow of slavery to become part of our national treasure? If the battle had been lost, or avoided, how long would the South have maintained slavery? As long as South Africa accepted apartheid? What would a Confederate victory have meant in the larger historical view? Would our two nations have been able to unite sufficiently to counter the threats of two world wars and communism? Who is to say that the North American continent would not have been divided again and again into many separate countries much like Europe? Do we truly appreciate the fact that we in the north do not need passports to go to Disney World? What would such a division have meant for travel, commerce, the postal service and defense?

No one should want to use violence, but everyone should have a fighting spirit when it comes to the defense of justice. Such nobility of character explains how a mild mannered Illinois lawyer, a family man and gentleman, a "nerd" if you will, like Abe Lincoln, could turn into such an advocate of fighting that his detractors would call him a "war lover." Yet, Lincoln did not throw himself and the nation impulsively into war. He tried every maneuver he had as a politician to settle the question without bloodshed. It was the South that finally brought the conflict onto the field. Once in the contest, however, Lincoln held nothing back. Even when his generals refused to confront the enemy, Lincoln never wavered. His determination and endurance finally won the day and saved the Union to realize her destiny as the last, best hope of the earth.

"True enough," you could say, "the nation faced a great crisis. Thank God, Lincoln saw the danger. Thank God he pushed the war effort. But thank God, greater still, that we do not live in such an age." But we do live in such an age. The blood of forty million Americans cries to us from the ground. If we could but remove the wax of moral turpitude from our ears, we would hear a battle hymn of freedom sharper and more insistent than it ever was during those dramatic years surrounding the Civil War. The time is once again ripe for heroes.

I have written this book because I love my country and, like so many of my countrymen, I seek a way to leave for the next generation an America that has moved one step further towards the realization of the noble ideals expressed by our forbears in the Declaration of Independence and the Constitution. My interest in the Civil War opened up for me an avenue by which we can rediscover the key virtues that were once our nation's saving grace. All Americans can rightly be proud of these virtues and should disdain the foul residue that is left wherever they are lacking.

I do not present this work as a polished historical account of the Civil War, but rather, as a meditation on the fundamental lessons that may guide our choices and inspire our leaders. We need to spell out clearly the astounding parallels between that first great threat to our nation's existence and the one created by legalized abortion in our time.

Whether or not you are a Civil War buff, this book is for you. All that is required is a sincere desire to find the true basis of our liberty and union. Together, we will take another look at the famous men and events that have become part of our national consciousness. We will do so, however, without the filtering of value-free spectacles. Turning our gaze from past to present, we will be able to see the reflection of those events near at hand and draw the necessary conclusions. I hope every reader will grasp the contradiction implied in an outlook that takes pride in our country as a free nation, while at the same time accepting the divisive philosophy embodied in the 1973 Supreme Court decision of *Roe v. Wade.*

In addition, I wish to illustrate in these pages how the conversion and subsequent moral fortitude of one man was responsible for saving the United States of America and strengthening for all time her position as a beacon of justice among the nations of the earth. I hope to make clear the cowardice that underlies the so-called moderate position held by politicians today in regard to the abortion question, and the promise of history's favorable judgement upon those who have the courage to be today's radicals. Perhaps this reflection will rekindle some of the passion and fighting spirit that was part of the Lincoln legacy.

Lastly, by pointing out the similarities between two great national movements for freedom, abolition and pro-life, I hope to give consolation and encouragement to those who have fought for so long and so thanklessly in defense of the unborn child. Their day will come.

You will find the vast majority of my historical facts are taken from David Herbert Donald's *Lincoln*. His two-time claim of the Pulitzer Prize is well deserved. Every now and then, you read a book that is so well written and captivating that in addition to stimulating an intellectual appetite it moves one to action. Donald's *Lincoln* was such as experience for me, a kind of call to arms, which has caused me to write this book. I sincerely hope that what I offer in these pages will build a worthy edifice upon his solid foundation.

Part I

The Ashes That Still Remain

His thoughtfulness for those who bore the brunt of the battles, his harmonious family relations, his absorbing love for his children, his anxiety for the well-being and conduct of the emancipated colored people, his unwavering faith in the hastening doom of human slavery, his affectionate regard for "the simple people," his patience, his endurance, his mental sufferings, and what he did for the Nation and for Humanity and Liberty — these all must be left to the systematic and enduring labors of the historian: Noah Brooks, *Lincoln Observed*

The Conversion of a President

Every Civil War buff knows three things about Abraham Lincoln: he agonized over the Civil War; he did not want to make slavery the central issue; he wrote, signed, and stood by the Emancipation Proclamation. An obvious tension lies between these last two. How did the war "become" about slavery? What brought the President's personal beliefs to the forefront, so much so that he had the courage to shape society by them? Here, indeed, is a conversion story — perhaps the most important conversion in the nation's history.

Conversion comes from a Latin word meaning "to turn" and is commonly used to describe a change of heart on a subject. A conversion can be over a great matter, such as the adoption of a new religious system, or a simple matter, such as a change in habit or opinion. It can be as sudden as St. Paul's falling from his horse, or the final culmination of a series of revelations. In either case, conversion always implies action. It is not just a change of mind, but a change of life. Conversion, then, leads to witness, for while we may not know a man's thoughts, we can usually judge his intentions by his actions.

The conversion of Abraham Lincoln from political moderate to leader satisfies all the criteria of a genuine conversion. Lincoln's career, his writings, and especially the words of others about him, reveal a man uniquely gifted to advance in understanding and determine his own course, not merely in the accommodating fashion of the politician, but as a human being rising steadily and courageously towards the highest ideals.

Following closely the path marked out by David Herbert Donald in *Lincoln*, I believe we can identify six specific stages of Lincoln's spiritual development:

(1) The earliest is that of the frontiersman raised in poverty and hard manual labor, close to both the beauty and cruelty of nature. From an early age he knew the grievous sorrow of personal loss and the resilience of pioneer hopes. These were the years that set in place the character of the man and formed in him deep values of diligence, invention, and human solidarity.

(2) Lincoln's entry into the political arena and legal profession marks the next stage in his development and the beginning of his lifelong courtship of justice. Longing to make his mark on the world and do something of lasting significance in mens' eyes, he finds direction for both his personal and professional life by a somewhat religious devotion to reason and law.

(3) Lincoln's next step forward is the result of the Kansas-Nebraska Act of 1854. Now a shrewd politician, Lincoln opts for the moderate position to restrict slavery's expansion rather than wipe it out immediately. He distrusts the radical abolitionists who maintain that there is a law higher than the Constitution and rests confident that by faithful observance to Constitutional law slavery will gradually be eliminated.

(4) This confidence, however, is shattered by the *Dred Scott* decision of 1857. Thrust now into a radical re-evaluation of his beliefs, Lincoln concludes that the Union the Founding Fathers desired is older than the Constitution and rests on the assumption of fundamental human rights. Preserving the

Union, now unequivocally linked in Lincoln's mind to liberty for all, becomes his greatest goal.

(5) Finally, faced with a war far bloodier and longer than anyone could have imagined, Lincoln's conversion is complete. Arriving at the conclusion that slavery is an internal cancer manifesting itself externally as secession, he takes the final step from moderate to leader and issues the Emancipation Proclamation.

(6) The last stage of Lincoln's conversion is more result than development. From the moment that he decides for immediate emancipation, Lincoln is a man in possession of himself and his country. His efforts to bind the nation's wounds and ensure a just reconstruction for the South could only be stopped by an assassin's bullet.

Let us recall the simple highlights of Lincoln's life to seek through these facts the interior movement of the man in the hope that we may identify with him at some stage and allow ourselves to move as he did from a position of compromise to decision.

Raised on the Frontier

Abraham Lincoln was born on February 12, 1809 in what is now Larue, Kentucky. His father, Thomas Lincoln, was a struggling frontier farmer who moved his family frequently in the hope of finding fertile ground. Little is known of Lincoln's mother, Nancy Hanks Lincoln. Prior to Abraham, she had given birth to Sarah in 1807. Abraham's younger brother, Thomas, would die in infancy. The Lincolns struggled to survive in the wilderness. From Kentucky they moved to Indiana, and from there to Illinois. At times, home was nothing more than a three-sided log structure and they went long stretches of time isolated from their neighbors. From the age of eight Abraham was assisting his father with the work of the farm and, by his own admission, grew up with an axe in his hand.

Lincoln probably first came into contact with slavery after the family moved to Knob Creek, Kentucky, near the old Cumberland Trail from Louisville to Nashville. Here he would have seen many passing by — settlers, peddlers, circuit-riding preachers, and slave traders with their merchandise in tow. The small, poor farms of Lincoln's region could not afford to use slaves and this, coupled with a strong strain of Baptist faith, made for an area largely opposed to slavery.

In 1818, Lincoln's mother Nancy succumbed to an epidemic of milk sickness that also claimed the lives of his aunt and uncle. Thomas Lincoln, unable to meet the demands of family and work alone, journeyed to Elizabethtown to find a wife. He married Sarah Bush Johnston, a hard working, good-hearted widow with three children. This was a turning point for the young Abraham who found in Sarah a friend and encouraging voice. Under her influence, he returned to school and learned to read, write, and "cipher to the Rule of Three." More than anything else, her affection and confidence helped to spur him on to better things.

None the less, Lincoln had little opportunity for education or cultural refinement. His formal schooling would amount to no more than a year. Yet, he read constantly and was known to walk miles to obtain a book. He would copy favorite selections onto boards or the rare sheet of paper, and commit it to memory. The things he accomplished virtually on his own attest to his native intelligence and high degree of personal motivation. He made of himself an educated man whose carefully crafted writing would eventually enrich the classics of American composition.

By law, Abraham was bound to serve his father and give all his earnings over to him until he was of legal age. Thomas Lincoln made good use of his son on his own land and sometimes hired him out to split rails for other farmers. Lincoln also brought home earnings from his work as a ferryman on the Ohio River. At the age of nineteen he took a flatboat of cargo down to the thriving port of New Orleans. This contact with the larger world made one thing crystal clear: Abraham would not be satisfied to follow in his father's footsteps in frontier farming.

As soon as he was able, Abraham set out on his own. He worked many kinds of jobs over the next few years and finally settled in New Salem on the Sangamon River. He became manager of a local store, as well as the lumber and grain mills. His first entry into the public arena came in the form of the local debating club. Lincoln took advantage of an opportunity to study grammar with the local schoolmaster and learned to love the works of Shakespeare and Robert Burns. The outstanding thing about Lincoln during this period was his facility at making friends. In addition to a gift for storytelling, his honesty, kindness, and good humor won the affection and trust of his community.

In 1832 Lincoln briefly served in the Black Hawk War. After an unsuccessful bid for the state legislature, he tried his hand at owning a store, but despite a conscientious effort, the business failed leaving him severely in debt. Lincoln's many friends guaranteed that he would find a job. He applied himself to learning the craft of surveying, and this plus the position of postmaster helped him eke out a living.

Abraham Lincoln had found his place in the community of New Salem, Illinois. He had seen difficult times, but had proved himself with his integrity and hard work. He was eager to be actively involved in the future of his community and his state. The heart of the public servant began to beat within him and he turned his attention to the world of politics. In 1834, at the age of twenty-five, Abraham Lincoln won his first seat in the Illinois Legislature.

Lincoln and the Law

Just a few years before his election, Lincoln had considered a career in law but decided that an uneducated man such as himself could never succeed. Subsequent experience on juries and lending a hand with the paralegal matters of his surveying work introduced Lincoln to many lawyers who were self-made men. Lincoln believed he could do as good if not better. He studied for the bar and received his license on September 9, 1836. In 1837 he moved to Springfield, Illinois, and entered into the first of several partnerships. Like most lawyers of the time, for several months every year he was required to travel about the region with a circuit judge. This exhausting work had a positive side for Lincoln's political career: it put him in contact with many kinds of people and gave him a good understanding of their needs and opinions.

Lincoln's 1834 term in the legislature was followed by subsequent terms in 1836, 1838, and 1840. He was a dedicated and hardworking member of the Whig party and would remain so until the party's dissolution in the late 1850's. Most of the work of the legislature concerned state business. Following an outburst of abolitionist agitation, however, Lincoln and a colleague, Dan Stone, defined their position on slavery and their opinion of abolitionists: "[Slavery] was founded on both injustice and bad policy, but that the promulgation of abolition tends rather to increase than abate its evils." Lincoln's distrust and dislike of abolitionist activity would be a recurrent theme in his political life. He believed that abolitionist extremes caused disruption of life and commerce and threatened the stability of established and effective legal procedures. While sharing abolitionist belief on the evil of slavery and its necessary demise, Lincoln placed domestic peace higher than the immediate extinction of slavery.

In Lincoln's early years as an Illinois lawyer, the frequent stories in the daily papers of violence, particularly that provoked by the slavery question, caused him to proclaim in no uncertain terms his love for law and the democratic process. He saw loss of such love as the key to lawlessness. In a statement delivered after a mulatto man in St. Louis was burned to death in mob-style violence, Lincoln said:

> *Let every American, every lover of liberty, every well-wisher to his posterity, swear by the blood of the Revolution, never to violate in the least*

particular the laws of the country; and never to tolerate their violation by others . . . Let reverence for the laws, be breathed by every American mother, to the lisping babe, that prattles on her lap — let it be taught in schools, in seminaries, and in colleges; — let it be written in Primers, spelling books, and in Almanacs; let it be preached from the pulpit, proclaimed in legislative halls, and enforced in courts of justice. In short, let it become the political religion of the nation.[1]

Young Mr. Lincoln also had personal reasons for loving the law as he did: "The earnestness of Lincoln's efforts to impose rationality on public life reflected his intense internal struggle to bring coherence to his own, still unshaped personality."[2] In a speech to the Washington Society in 1842, on the subject of prohibition, he pointed to uncontrolled passion as the real root of social evil and proposed in its place "reason, cold, calculating, unimpassioned reason . . . mind, all conquering mind, shall live and move the monarch of the world. Glorious consummation! Hail fall of Fury! Reign of Reason, all hail!"[3]

Lincoln's attachment to reason could not prevent him from falling in love. After a long and turbulent courtship, he married Mary Todd on November 4, 1842. Nearly nine months to the day, Robert Todd Lincoln was born. The Lincolns's marriage had its challenges, but their love and fidelity to one another was obvious. Although the young couple started out with the simplest means, Mary's wealthy and socially prominent family afforded her husband an avenue of entry into a higher social level. This, coupled with Lincoln's own ambition and exceptional abilities, helped them improve their situation.

---

1. David Herbert Donald, *Lincoln* (New York, NY: Simon & Schuster, 1996), pp. 80-81
2. Donald, *Lincoln*, p. 83
3. Donald, *Lincoln*, p. 82

In 1846 Lincoln won his bid for the United States Congress, his one and only experience of Washington politics prior to becoming president fourteen years later. His term was not marked by extraordinary achievement, but he did make certain statements that a few years later he would have to defend. In the debate over lands taken from Mexico, for example, Lincoln defended the right of a people to revolt:

> *Any people anywhere . . . have the right to rise up, and shake off the existing government, and form a new one that suits them better . . . Any portion of such people that can, may revolutionize, and make their own, of so much of the territory as they inhabit . . . This is a most valuable, — a most sacred right — a right, which we hope and believe, is to liberate the world.* "[4]

More importantly, when the annexation of territories gained from Mexico became an issue, Lincoln supported the Wilmot Proviso[5] and other measures seeking to confine slavery to the states were it already existed. While personally opposed to the institution, he did not want to align himself with the abolitionists whose appeal to something higher than the law distressed and frightened him. He opted, instead, for a moderate position that sought to deal with slavery gradually by restricting it to the states where it already existed. This stand would allow him to be somewhat palatable to both sides of the question — a clever ploy for an ambitious politician.

Lincoln had very little personal exposure to slavery, but during his time in Washington he did make the acquaintance of abolitionists. These men opened his eyes to the true nature of slavery — no small step on his way to conversion:

---

4. Donald, *Lincoln*, p. 128
5. The Wilmot Proviso was authored by David Wilmot of Pennsylvania and provided that slavery would be prohibited from all territories gained in the Mexican War.

He had all along been against the peculiar institution, but it had not hitherto seemed a particularly important or divisive issue, partly because he had so little personal knowledge of slavery. But in Washington, his strongly antislavery friends in Congress, like Joshua R. Giddings and Horace Mann, helped him see that the atrocities that occurred every day in the national capital were the inevitable results of the slave system. As Lincoln's sensitivity to the cruelty of slavery changed, so did his memories. In 1841, returning from the Speed plantation, he had been amused by the cheerful docility of a gang of African-Americans who were being sold down the Mississippi. Now, reflecting on that scene, he recalled it as "a continual torment," which crucified his feelings.[6]

During this same period, Lincoln closely followed events in Kentucky where his father-in-law, Robert S. Todd, and Henry Clay were working for the gradual emancipation of the slaves. All their efforts failed. Todd himself died before realizing the defeat of his bid for the senate. Lincoln was brought to the stark awareness that slavery was not just a matter of social institution and economic necessity. Some men enjoyed slavery. As a young Kentuckian told him, "You might have any amount of land; money in your pocket or bank stock and while travelling around nobody would be any wiser, but if you had a darkey trudging at your heels everybody would see him and know that you owned slaves."[7]

No doubt, for the kindly and generous hearted Lincoln, this realization of the cruelty and human malice behind slavery was shocking. The picture of slavery that Lincoln had received from his wife's family was a fairly pleasant one. In comparison with other

---

6. Donald, *Lincoln*, pp. 165-166
7. Donald, *Lincoln*, p. 166

slave owners, they were very good to their slaves, many of whom were integral parts of the family, much like Mammy in Gone with the Wind. Such a "nice experience" of slavery worked against the slaves' emancipation since it masked the horror of the institution. Lincoln remarked that it was at the slave markets in Washington, D.C. where he first saw the ugly side of slavery.

The fact that Lincoln married Mary, who had been brought up in "style" complete with slaves, would often be used against him during the war to question his loyalty to the Union cause. It was a tie he could not deny. Most of Mary's relatives and friends were Southerners and slave owners; in fact, the commander-in-chief of the United States had as a brother-in-law a general in the Confederacy. When the general's wife stopped in to visit her sister in the White House, tongues started wagging. Mary Todd Lincoln readily admitted she did not understand the abolitionists, but she stuck firmly by her husband in his anti-slavery convictions.

Lincoln, like most men of his time, could not envision the successful integration of black freedmen in a white society. He decided on colonization of African-Americans to Liberia as the most reasonable way of dealing with the problem. Even Donald calls Lincoln's colonization plan "a very useful escape."[8] Yet, we must be careful not to judge Lincoln too harshly. While it may seem a preposterous suggestion to us now, he was seeking what he believed to be the fairest, kindest plan for a people unprepared by education or culture to enter a white society. He was also acknowledging the strength and maliciousness of an almost invincible prejudice.

In 1848 Lincoln helped to bring about the election of General Zachary Taylor as president. However, failing to achieve the reward of a plum government position, he settled back into his Springfield routine, disillusioned and tormented by a sense of personal failure. For the next six years his life revolved around his

---

8. Donald, *Lincoln*, p. 167

successful law practice. He turned to self-improvement to further his ends, even mastering the six books of Euclid, and kept a hand in public speaking by giving circuit lectures. He remained active in party politics and kept his eyes open for some opportunity to serve his country.

The Moderate Platform

Lincoln had evolved as a politician. He knew how to read the signs of the times and how to wait. An insight into Lincoln's political savvy is afforded us in the advice he gave to Richard Yates, a young Whig seeking election to Lincoln's former congressional seat. The major issue of the time was the annexation of territories won from Mexico. Would they be slave or free? Lincoln advised Yates to remain "cautiously noncommittal" and maintain that "of all political objects the preservation of the Union stands number one." While supporting the Wilmot Proviso and the Compromise of 1850,[9] he should make clear his opposition to the extension of slavery.[10]

Clearly, Lincoln knew just how to walk the middle of the road with voters. He had mastered the art of pleasing all sides.

The Kansas-Nebraska Act of 1854 was the event that brought Lincoln back into the spotlight. The great territory of Nebraska was near to entering the union. Would it be free or slave? Theoretically, the issue had already been resolved. According to the Missouri Compromise, Nebraska was to be a free territory. But when chairman of the Senate Committee on Territories, Illinois state senator Stephen A. Douglas, put forth a bill to establish a territorial government in Nebraska, with the exclusion of slavery as part and

---

9. The Compromise of 1850 admitted California as a free state and gave to the inhabitants of the New Mexico and Utah territories the right to decide for themselves about slavery. It also created a tough new fugitive slave law.
10. Donald, *Lincoln*, pp. 162-163

parcel; southern voices rose in protest. The admission of Nebraska as a free territory represented to the South the growing power of abolitionists and Northern interests in the federal government. Douglas hoped to get around the problem by encouraging the practice of "popular sovereignty" — in other words, let the people of the territory decide, just as New Mexico and Utah had done in accordance with the Compromise of 1850. He also agreed to the dividing of Nebraska into two territories, Nebraska and Kansas, with the understanding that Kansas would end up being a slave territory, thus balancing things out.

The Kansas-Nebraska Act of 1854 was a watershed locally and politically. It set off a conflagration in the territories as opponents and proponents of slavery shipped into the area large numbers of their members to swing the polls. Armed conflict broke out, the most famous of which was John Brown's brutal murder of pro-slavery settlers at Pottawatomie Creek. The utter rejection of the Missouri Compromise that the Kansas-Nebraska Act entailed was a stunning blow to abolitionists and a serious goading to Northern pride. The South had agreed to the Missouri Compromise — what right did they have to go back on it now? Evidently, slavery was not scheduled for gradual extinction, but for perpetuity. The introduction of new states made the simple "let things be the way they are" attitude most impractical.

Lincoln was at first quiet about the Kansas-Nebraska Act. He astutely waited until the time was right for his reentry on the political scene. He took to the road again purportedly as an advocate of Richard Yates's reelection to Congress, careful to avoid any "radical" tags. He was just a Whig campaigning for a fellow Whig. In attacking the Kansas-Nebraska Act, Lincoln refined his previously held moderate line between radical abolitionists and Southern secessionists. Simply put, he stood for a restriction of slavery. The practice was not to be permitted to expand. He advocated any measures that would encourage presently slave-holding states to voluntarily cease the practice. Such measures might include financial compensation for slaves released, and the colonization of freed blacks outside of the United States.

Lincoln still considered slavery a secondary issue, an uncomfortable and inconvenient reality, but certainly not an evil plant to be pulled up roots and all. His hesitation to fully engage in the newly formed Republican Party illustrates this point. He wanted it clear that he was speaking against the Kansas-Nebraska Act as a Whig, not a Republican and certainly not an abolitionist. He would, he admitted, allow the extension of slavery "rather than see the Union dissolved." In short, he was a master moderate, playing it safe and close to the hip. He was adamantly opposed to any kind of armed conflict. He considered any kind of fighting wrong and unconstitutional and encouraged abolitionists to think of "other more effective channels" of action.[11] He had no fighting spirit for the cause of emancipation.

One effect of the Kansas-Nebraska Act controversy, however, was the final disintegration of the Whig Party. Anti-slavery Whigs and Democrats and various independents began to come together to form a new party. Lincoln was cool at first to the idea, but recognizing the reality that political life meant membership in a political party, he threw himself into the formation of the Republican Party, becoming one of its chief architects and its leading spokesman in Illinois.

Although Lincoln had found a voice in the controversy over Kansas-Nebraska, and established a national forum for his ideas by taking a prominent position in the Republican Party, his position still left him a somewhat shadowy figure in the public mind. What exactly did he represent? He insisted on his opposition to the *extension* of slavery only. Thus, he could find some favor with both Southern Democrats and Northern abolitionists, but both parties could also find enough in him to distrust. He lacked that singleness of vision that would set him apart from other politicians holding the

---

11. Donald, *Lincoln*, p. 188

moderate line. He was defeated for the senate race in 1855 and failed to find a place on the Republican ticket of 1856. He returned home to a year of law practice. Once again, he was out of the limelight and his political future seemed dubious.

Emergence of a Moral Force

In the late 1850's, arguments between North and South took a surprising turn. Instead of arguing for slavery as a necessary evil, Southern slaveholders started promoting slavery as a positive good. Lincoln wryly responded, "Although volume upon volume is written to prove slavery a very good thing, we never hear of the man who wished to take the good of it, *by being a slave himself.*" Still, the change in argument reflected a deepening of the error into which the nation had fallen. Truth was becoming a rare commodity as language was more and more abused. It was perhaps inevitable that even the highest court in the land would become a rhetoric mill for injustice.

Lincoln had a great reverence for the United States Constitution and believed with all his heart that adhering to the system laid down by the nation's founders would lead to the ultimate victory of right over wrong. He somewhat naively placed his full confidence in this system:

> *He had enormous respect for the law and for the judicial process. He felt these offered a standard of rationality badly needed in a society threatened, on the one side, by the unreasoning populism of the Democrats, who believed that the majority was always right, and the equally unreasonable moral absolutism of reformers like the abolitionists, who appealed to a higher law than even the Constitution. As recently as the 1856 campaign he had invoked the judiciary as the ultimate arbiter of disputes over slavery. "The Supreme Court of the United States is the tribunal to decide such questions . . . We will*

> ***submit to its decisions, and if you, [the Democrats]
> do also, there will be an end of the matter.***"[12]

Yet, Lincoln had fallen into a fundamental error in his political thinking. The law alone is not sufficient to heal society's ills. Though his love for the Constitution was laudable, his understanding of that noble document was as yet undeveloped. He did not understand that justice is prior to all written law.

The event that jolted Lincoln out of his legalistic myopia was the 1857 Supreme Court decision in the *Dred Scott* case. In an opinion authored by Chief Justice Roger B. Taney, the court declared that African-Americans were not and could not be citizens of the United States. The founders of the country had never intended the rights enumerated in the Declaration of Independence for the black man. In brutal language, Taney asserted that a black man had no rights which a white man was bound to respect. Furthermore, U.S. laws prohibiting slavery in the territories were unconstitutional — in fact, the federal government had no power to affect slavery in the states or territories.

Lincoln was stunned. The obvious error of the Court's decision and Justice Taney's opinion in particular caused Lincoln to move from an unqualified attachment to the Constitution toward the *a priori* principles of the Declaration of Independence. He began to understand that these unwritten principles must support all written law. What he had so feared in abolitionist thinking, he now recognized as true. Though he could not as yet see how freedom for all would become a working reality in American society, he could at least appreciate that a people devoid of a love of liberty, the first and foremost of the Declaration's principles, would never succeed in passing just laws.

His heart was sickened by Taney's "obvious violence to the plain unmistakable language of the Declaration." He was amazed at the extent to which some men would go to ensure the

---

12. Donald, *Lincoln*, p. 200

continuance of slavery: "Now in order to make Negro slavery eternal and universal, the Declaration 'is assailed, and sneered at, and construed, and hawked at, and torn, till, if its framers could rise from their graves, they could not at all recognize it.' So blatant was the Chief Justice's misreading of the law, so gross was his distortion of the documents fundamental to American liberty, that Lincoln's faith in an impartial, rational judiciary was shaken, never again did he give deference to the rulings of the Supreme Court."[13]

Suddenly, Lincoln's sensitive nature, always moved by the suffering of the innocent or defenseless, began to recognize the true nature of the plight of his fellow Americans in chains. He could see for the first time the impossibility of the slaves' situation, the almost insurmountable wall of legal jargon and social prejudice that hemmed them in on all sides. He went as far as to accuse the Chief Justice of working together with other Democrats to extend and perpetuate slavery. In eloquent words, Lincoln gave vent to his sympathy and sorrow:

> *All the powers of earth seem rapidly combining against him ... They have him in his prison house; they have searched his person, and left no prying instrument with him. One after another they have closed the heavy iron doors upon him, and now they have him, as it were, bolted in with a lock of a hundred keys, which can never be unlocked without the concurrence of every key; the keys in the hands of a hundred different men, and they are scattered to a hundred different distant places; and they stand musing as to what invention, in all the dominions of mind and matter, can be produced to make the impossibility of his escape more complete than it is.*[14]

Taking refuge in the belief that court decisions could be

---

13. Donald, *Lincoln*, p. 201
14. Donald, *Lincoln*, p. 201

overturned, Lincoln felt free to denounce the *Dred Scott* decision. "We know the court that made it, has often over-ruled its own decisions, and we shall do what we can to have it to over-rule this." At the same time, this peace loving and patient man would respect due process: "We offer no *resistance* to it."[15] In saying this, he placed himself in direct contrast to radical abolitionists and pro-slavery parties who were poised to do violence to protect their agendas regardless of the law.

The period following the *Dred Scott* decision saw the emergence of Abraham Lincoln as a new man — driven not so much by party politics and ambition as by a moral imperative. There were others toting the abolitionist platform, but none had the ring of sincerity and straightforwardness of Abraham Lincoln. This came out clearly in his famous debates with Stephen A. Douglas while they jousted for a seat in the Senate in 1858. From the first, he made clear his conviction that slavery and freedom could not exist side by side: "*A house divided against itself cannot stand . . . I believe this government cannot endure permanently half slave and half free.*"[16] In opposition to Douglas's stand on racial inequality and popular sovereignty, Lincoln insisted that slavery was a moral issue that had to be resolved according to the principles of equality and freedom laid down by the Founding Fathers. They had not wanted slavery, but tolerated it, hoping for its eventual demise by prohibiting its growth.

Although the sincerity and commitment of Lincoln to the ideal of liberty are evident in his speeches and the Lincoln-Douglas debates, he demonstrated a yet undeveloped appreciation for the black man as an equal. The man who would go down in history as the great emancipator of the slaves sometimes spoke in shockingly racist terms. Debating with the hard-hitting, up front racist Douglas in Charleston, Lincoln found himself saying: "I am not, nor ever have been in favor of bringing about in any way the social and political equality of the white and black races . . . I am not nor ever

15. Donald, *Lincoln*, p. 201
16. Donald, *Lincoln*, p. 207

have been in favor of making voters or jurors of negroes, nor of qualifying them to hold office, nor to intermarry with white people . . . There is a physical difference between the white and black races which I believe will forever forbid the two races living together on terms of social and political equality."[17]

However, even with declarations such as this, we have some reason to believe that Lincoln's heart truly was not in such a claim. He always avoided such negative comments in his prepared speeches, and wanted to do so on this occasion had he not been duped by a cunning reporter. He was also a politician, trying to win the favor of many by showing himself in agreement with commonly held points of view on the differences between the races. Author Donald E. Fehrenbacher points out that a closer look at Lincoln's words on this occasion reveals the more positive meaning he had underneath: "'He conceded that the Negro *might not* be his equal, or he said that the Negro *was not* his equal *in certain respects.*' Even when he agreed that blacks did not have the same civil rights as whites, he nearly always added in the next breath that they were the equal of whites in the enjoyment of the natural rights pledged in the Declaration of Independence."[18]

Lincoln was, after all, a man of his times. He believed fiercely in the traditions and practices of the American people, meaning a white people; hence, he could not see his way to a society in which blacks and whites lived as equals. He preferred colonization to integration. It cannot be emphasized enough that Lincoln's final conversion involved not only a developed sense of the proper weight of the Constitution, but the personhood of the African-American as well.

Douglas won the senate race of 1858 and Lincoln returned to Springfield once again, but the national exposure that he had

---

17. Donald, *Lincoln*, p. 221
18. Donald, *Lincoln*, endnote p. 633, from Donald E. Fehrenbacher, Only His Stepchildren, Lincoln in Text and Context (Stanford, CA: Stanford University Press, 1987), p. 106

gained in the debates with Douglas placed him in good stead for his party's nomination in the next presidential election. He prepared for that event with a series of speaking engagements in the Northeast where he was greeted with enthusiasm. In the Republican convention of 1860, Lincoln had the clear majority of his party. A split in the Democratic Party between Douglas and John C. Breckinridge guaranteed Lincoln's election to the presidency. While Douglas had succeeded in winning the battles, Lincoln would win the war.

Republican President

In the winter of 1861, the crisis between North and South reached a climax. Lincoln's election was the catalyst for a final break. On December 20, 1860, South Carolina's representatives voted to secede from the Union. The states of Florida, Mississippi, Alabama, Georgia and Louisiana quickly followed suit. Soon Texas was showing secession activity. On February 4, 1861, a month before Lincoln's inauguration, six Southern states sent representatives to Montgomery, Alabama to set up a new government with Jefferson Davis of Mississippi at its head. Federal forts and arsenals within these states were seized by the Confederacy leaving only two major Union strongholds still unclaimed, Fort Pickens in Pensacola and Fort Sumter in South Carolina. At 4:30am on April 12, 1861, Confederate forces fired upon Fort Sumter and the rest, as they say, is history.

Throughout the winter, Congress had set about finding a last minute compromise on the issue of slavery. In December 1860 Senator John J. Crittenden of Kentucky proposed an agreement by which the Missouri Compromise would be extended westward, all the way to the Pacific, with territories to the north of the line prohibiting slavery and territories to the south of the line permitting it. Future states would be free to decide the issue as they entered the Union. In addition, the Crittenden Compromise asserted that the Constitution could never be amended to give Congress power over slavery in any state. It also strengthened the Fugitive Slave

Act and provided Federal funds to compensate slave owners whose slaves got away.

The Crittenden Compromise was tantalizing, but it provided only a quick fix for the immediate problem while offering no permanent solution. It promised to preserve the Union by buying some time to resolve the slavery question in a legal and peaceful way. At the same time it allowed things to just go on being they way they always had been, but on a bigger scale. The heated debate surrounding Crittenden's compromise manifests the centrality of slavery as the "material cause" of the debate over states' rights. The South was interested in their state rights not in some abstract philosophical way. Freedom is never purely abstract; it exists in the freedom to do this or that. The South defended their rights because they were interested in preserving a system that guaranteed them significant profits.

President-elect Lincoln could have taken a stand which would have won over vacillating Republicans and caused the measure to be passed. He did not. On March 2, 1861, Crittenden's plan was narrowly defeated in the Senate. Lincoln's rejection of the Crittenden Compromise put him at odds with other Republicans, but he held firm to the party platform on which he had run and been elected: opposition to the extension of slavery. In the President's first inaugural address, he vowed to follow this path and do nothing to interfere with the domestic policies of the states.

Personal factors must certainly have played a part in President-elect Lincoln's assessment of the Crittenden Compromise. The senator was closely associated with both the Lincoln and Todd families and had been one of Lincoln's early political heroes. At one time, Crittenden had been willing to recommend Lincoln for a cabinet position for President Taylor. "There is Lincoln whom I regard as a rising man — if he were an applicant I would go for him." Loyalty and friendship were at stake as well as political policy. On the other hand, not all Lincoln's memories of the senator were good ones. In the senatorial elections of 1858, Crittenden surprised Lincoln by throwing his support behind Douglas as an affirmation of "popular rights and public justice." His action had serious ramifications for the young Republican Party, sending many former Whigs and borderline Republicans over to the Democrats. As one of the architects of the Republican Party, Lincoln had something to grind an axe about.

But it was not personal considerations that moved Lincoln against the compromise. Nor was it the result of a firm and final stand on emancipation, for again, he held to a moderate position in which he could hold up "saving the Union" as his standard. Rather, Lincoln believed that such a compromise would be selling out on the Union. In essence, the Southern states would succeed in their ambition to change the *form* of the government — something that could only be done legally by amending the Constitution. In the words of Donald: "Lincoln's commitment to maintaining the Union was absolute. As a young man, he had looked to reason for guidance, both in his turbulent emotional life and in the disorderly society in which he grew up. When that proved inadequate, he found stability in the law and in the Constitution, but after the Dred Scott decision, he could no longer have unqualified faith in either. The concept of the Union, older than the Constitution, deriving from the Declaration of Independence with its promise of liberty for all, had become the premise on which all his other political beliefs rested."[19]

Lincoln had had enough of playing games with the South. In opting for secession, they had pressed the one button that would move him into action more than any other: they had deviated from the Constitution. If monarchies are subject to the possibility of despotism, democracies are subject to the danger of one group adopting the adage "might makes right," the playground rule of the bully. Lincoln was not going to watch the South play bully to the Union. They were to play fair or not play at all.

---

19. Donald, *Lincoln*, p. 269

From the first shots of Fort Sumter until the spring of 1865, Abraham Lincoln set one and only one goal before his eyes as commander-in-chief: preserve the Union. He had personally acknowledged the evil of slavery and the necessity of eradicating it as soon as possible, but he had not yet moved to the position where his own personal morality would direct the course of a nation. He lifted his banner over the concept of "Union" and hoped that everyone understood, as he did, that Union was inseparable from freedom.

Holding the Moderate Line

Throughout the first phases of the war, Lincoln continued to insist that the real issue at stake was the preservation of the Union. He promised immediate reconciliation and full reinstatement to any state that would submit once again to the national authority. He resisted the constant pressuring of abolitionists to make of the war a crusade against slavery, hoping until the last moment that the Southern states would return to the Union on their own initiative, and that slavery would then be dealt with in accord with the laws of the land. Even in the face of pressure from his closest advisors, he would not allow slavery to be the central issue.

The President's position was the popular one of the moment. Shortly after the first battle of Bull Run, John J. Crittenden authored a senate resolution which served as a vote of confidence for President Lincoln: ". . . that this war is not waged . . . for any purpose of conquest or subjugation, nor purpose of overthrowing . . . established institutions [slavery] . . . but to defend . . . the Constitution and to preserve the Union." It is a poignant historical fact that Crittenden himself was a visible sign of the times with one son serving as a major general in the Union army, and another serving as a major general in the Confederate Army.

The embarrassing defeat of Bull Run had sent Senators Chandler and Sumner, together with Vice President Hamlin, to Lincoln with the request that the war be turned into a battle between slavery and freedom. "Lincoln listened politely but said such measures were too far in advance of public opinion."[20] Lincoln felt bound by the words of his inaugural address promising no interference with slavery, as well as the recently adopted Crittenden Resolution. His convictions about the evils of slavery did not yet equal his anger over the South's flagrant rejection of law and order. Occupied more by a desire for domestic tranquility, and not seeing the connection between peace and justice, he could turn his eyes away from the ugliness of the South's peculiar institution. He certainly believed government had the right to abolish slavery, but it ought not be exercised unless it was requested by the people.

Lincoln's response to Chandler, Sumner and Hamlin also contained a misunderstanding of representative government. He listens to a request by some rather powerful and influential people — then he tells them their request is denied because the people do not request it. The irony of this attitude needs to be spelled out. A good democratic leader must always be attentive to what the people are saying; but a great leader in a democracy knows it is just as important to which group of people he or she gives an ear. The voice of the many is not the sole deciding factor in a leader's choice. The voice of right and reason must also come into play. There may be moments when a leader stands alone, against the will of the majority, because he or she recognizes that what is demanded will not be good for the people. This is the courage proper to leaders. If not, than what need does a society have of leaders? The mathematical polling of votes alone could decide every issue with the result that a computer, not a person, could best do the job.

Lincoln's determination to maintain the moderate position and resist any hint of radical abolitionism is nowhere more clearly displayed than in his reprimand of General John Charles Frémont. In May 1861 Frémont replaced Brigadier General William A.

20. Fehrenbacher, *Lincoln in Text and Context*, p. 314

Harney in command of the Department of the West with his headquarters in St. Louis. He was no West Pointer, and his service had been with the topographical engineers rather than with the line. But it was his single-minded and self-initiated action in regards to slavery that caused his disfavor with the President.

In an attempt to deal with a Confederate invasion and ongoing guerilla warfare throughout his territory of command, Frémont proclaimed martial law in the entire state of Missouri. Civilians bearing arms would be tried by court-martial and shot if convicted, and the slaves of any person serving the Confederacy would be emancipated. From Frémont's point of view, the action was warranted. He had to deal with untrustworthy Confederate sympathizers all around him, as well as make up for a lack of men and supplies that was not forthcoming from Washington.

Lincoln's main concern was keeping the balance in the Border States. Frémont's proclamation swung that balance against the North by making slavery the fundamental issue of the war. Nowhere was the precariousness of the situation felt more than in Kentucky whose legislature was just moving to abandon neutrality and choose sides. Lincoln believed that "to lose Kentucky is nearly the same as to lose the whole game." Other states would have followed. Frémont had gone too far, too fast, and Lincoln pulled in the reigns. He asked Frémont to modify his proclamation, saying it "will alarm our Southern Union friends, and turn them against us — perhaps ruin our rather fair prospect for Kentucky."[21]

In defense of his position, Frémont sent his wife Jessie to Washington to hand deliver a letter of appeal. Mrs. Frémont augmented the letter by her own expression of belief that a blow must be struck against slavery so that the Union would gain British sentiment. Lincoln was neither cordial nor accommodating towards Mrs. Frémont. He met her

---

21. Donald, *Lincoln*, p. 315

immediately upon her arrival, not even allowing her time to rest and refresh herself. He offered her no chair. And in response to her views he cut her off with, "You are quite a female politician." No small slight for the daughter of Missouri Senator Thomas Hart Benton and wife of a one-time senator from California and first Republican candidate for president. Mrs. Frémont was certainly no stranger to political discussion. But Lincoln was irate that his cherished moderation had been undercut. He affirmed his conviction that the war was "for a great national idea, the Union, and . . . General Frémont should not have dragged the Negro into it."[22]

Ironically, Lincoln's criticism of Frémont was the very description of what he himself would do in a few years. He complained that "[General] Frémont's proclamation, as to confiscation of property, and the liberation of slaves, is *purely political*, and not within the range of *military* law, or necessity." The general assumed he "may do *anything* he pleases . . . Can it be pretended that it is any longer the government of the U.S. — any government of Constitution and laws — wherein a General, or a President, may make permanent rules of property by proclamation?"[23] By the end of 1862, Lincoln would change his view radically and be himself the author of such a proclamation.

From Moderate to Leader

Pinpointing a moment of conversion in someone's life is not an easy task. So many factors go into the making of that final passage from darkness to light, not the least of which is the assent of the individual. Abraham Lincoln had certainly come through the successive stages of a spiritual development that had prepared him

---

22. Donald, *Lincoln*, p. 315
23. Donald, *Lincoln*, p. 317

for this moment: his simple frontier upbringing with its values derived from nature and human solidarity; his sensitivity, so attuned to the suffering of the helpless and the innocent; his love of the law and appreciation for its role in a democratic society; his understanding that law itself must stand before a court of transcendent principles. The rail-splitter had himself been hewn for this moment.

In the years of Civil War and, in particular, the months leading up to the Emancipation Proclamation, there must have been those things that worked particularly well on the conscience of the President — things that caused him amazement, moved him to wonder, and ultimately gave him the courage to act. Even while he continued to hold a politically correct position, and do so with all the conviction of his principled nature, he could not ignore the cloud of witnesses which surrounded him.

It must have been a sobering and enlightening thing for him to hear about the exploits of the Irish Brigade, for example. Certainly news of their fighting spirit must have been music to his ears. The famous Holy Cross chaplain, whose statue stands on the Gettysburg battlefield as well as on the campus of Notre Dame, Father William Corby, gives us a little taste of what undoubtedly Lincoln must have heard in his countless hours in the telegraph room:

> . . .*"Jack Gasson," the wild Irishman. He was perfectly fearless. "What man can dare I dare, was his motto." No wonder the Confederates would cry out when they beheld the green flag: "Here comes that d---- green flag again." They knew the undaunted courage of the race, and had tested the same more than once. Withal, these very men were religious, and like children in church.*[24]

---

24. William Corby, C.S.C., *Memoirs of Chaplain Life* (New York, NY: Fordham University Press, 1992), p. 110

For a President who had no end of difficulties getting his generals onto the field, the courage of the Irish Brigade provided a contrast and comparison. Why were these men different? In his memoirs, Father Corby explains that many in the Irish Brigade were immigrants or sons of immigrants from Ireland, a country that had painfully experienced the submission of one people to another. Freedom would have a deeper meaning for them than for other Union soldiers. Perhaps "union" as an ideal was not enough to bind the country together. One had to shoot higher for men to give their lives.

Nor can we underestimate the continual insistence of abolitionists. Though uncomfortable with their radical program for societal change, Lincoln was a good and just man on whom their arguments would not be lost. The example of Mrs. Jessie Frémont and others must have worked steadily and quietly on his mind. This was another kind of courage on another kind of battlefield. One could easily dismiss the radical John Brown's of the world, but what of ordinary, loyal citizens who made great sacrifices for so long for such an unpopular cause?

As Lincoln watched the misery of war continue through months and then years, he must have delved deeper into the causes of the war. Union, so cherished and so longed for, began to settle herself slightly below her sister liberty. He could feel within himself the re-ordering of a belief system of a lifetime. Yet, to move from the position he had held with such passion for so long, something more was needed. Something had to open the heart of a president to admit the true nature of the nation's suffering and move him to radical measures. What was it that swung the balance in this man so devoted to "cool, calculating reason" and so adept at the political machine?

On July 13, 1863, Lincoln rode with William Seward and Gideon Welles to the funeral of Edwin Stanton's infant son. Sitting in that carriage, feeling the heavy hand of death and the injustice of a life snuffed out before its time, Abraham Lincoln moved from the sidelines to the center. He announced to his startled colleagues, "I have about come to the conclusion that we must free the slaves or be ourselves subdued."[25] The connection had been made. The survival of the Union hinged on the triumph of justice.

It is not a popular method these days to understand a man's actions by way of his heart. Those properly schooled in history would consider such an analysis too subjective. The trend of most modern historical efforts is to assume that truth is found only in that which can be observed and scientifically recorded. Rarely is the soul, that is to say, the entire person fully considered. There is emerging, however, a new "phenomenological approach" to knowledge that takes personal perspectives into account: "In any historical study, questions of "what caused x?" do not admit of simple answers. Human history is a very complex web of persons, convictions, memories, motivations, values, intentions, etc. Cause and effect does not operate in simple "x causes y" progression. "Y" occurs, because of the interplay of many factors and influences, operating at different levels and motivating particular acts. The story is never simple. Different aspects and sides of the question reveal themselves to one who "walks around" the concrete experience of a civil war breaking out."[26]

In those dark days, with no end in sight to the war, while Americans continued to slaughter one another wholesale, Lincoln's weary spirit must have been particularly sensitive to the funeral of Stanton's little, innocent child. The truly defining element of Lincoln's life was his love for his family. Biographers are unanimous in asserting his affection for his sons. The loss of Eddie in Springfield in 1850 had been devastating for Abraham and Mary. For fifty-two days they had had to watch their barely four-year-old son suffer the agony of pulmonary tuberculosis. Lincoln could not have been unaffected by the suffering of Stanton and his wife.

---

25. Donald, *Lincoln*, p. 362
26. Fr. Kevin Holmes, M.A., S.T.L., J.C.D., private interview, 1999

Death always calls forth an appreciation for the precious gift of life and raises the question of the ultimate meaning of human existence. But the death of a child has the unfathomable power to stop us in our tracks. It seems so unjust. A life well spent into old age and then returned to the earth from which it came has a kind of sense to it. But the death of one who has not realized his or her potential, who has not enjoyed all that life has to offer, seems to be without reason. An infant's tombstone of the 18th century expressed this mystery with black humor: "Since I was so soon done for, I wonder what I was begun for."

That day in the carriage with Seward and Welles, with the "why" of human suffering before him, Lincoln experienced solidarity, not only with the Stantons, but with all those who suffer. He felt for every soldier on the field in this terrible Civil War; he felt for every black man deprived of his basic human liberties. He felt a longing to act, to do something to relieve the human condition. He could do nothing for the child who had died, or his grieving parents, but he knew he held in his hands the fate of another man — the black man.

Many factors merged in that final moment of decision as Lincoln headed towards the funeral of Stanton's son. But I am convinced that ultimately it was Lincoln's humanity, his love for his family, and his responsiveness to human suffering that offers the key to his decision to proclaim emancipation. I am reminded of the final words of *The Jeweler's Shop*, a movie based on the play written by Pope John Paul II: "The history of the world passes through the family. It passes through love."

Events developed rapidly. While Seward and Welles begged the President to consider more carefully his decision, Lincoln was interested only in the practical details: how and when. He decided the most expedient route was to take advantage of the war powers that gave him certain rights over the property of citizens. He would issue an Emancipation Proclamation. In all fairness, he would offer the rebel states a chance to return to the Union before such a decree went into effect, knowing full well that this would not happen. He then waited for the right moment, trusting that if God wanted this action taken, he would himself reveal his will in a Union victory. That victory came with Antietam on September 17, 1862. Two days later he called his cabinet together and set before them the proposed Emancipation Proclamation which would take effect on January 1, 1863.

The Legacy of a Leader

Lincoln's conversion did not spend itself with the Emancipation Proclamation. From this point on he acted like a man freed from enslavement to political maneuvering and social convention. He took on the bearing of a true leader, and all those around him noted the change.

Lincoln had need of a new wellspring of courage in the days following the Proclamation. Things did not immediately improve; in fact, they grew darker. A massive defeat at Chancellorsville, followed by difficulties at Charleston, Vicksburg, eastern Tennessee and North Virginia were coupled with an ugly stir of criticism at home. Protests against the war became more vocal, with democrats suing for peace negotiations and accusing the President of incompetence at best and tyranny at worst. Lincoln found himself in the middle of two critical fronts — on the one side the Democrats clamoring for peace negotiations and on the other the radical Republicans wanting abolitionist generals.

Yet something had been unleashed in the President from the moment of the Emancipation Proclamation. In the face of crumbling public opinion, Lincoln took the unprecedented step of defending his actions in a series of public letters. First appearing in the *New York Tribune*, these letters were eventually printed and distributed by the Republican Party. In the end, 10,000,000 people read them. Lincoln made the national emergency clear and defended the decisions which had infringed on the freedom of speech and the press, allowed the arrest of dissenters, and necessitated his suspension of the writ of habeas corpus. When Missouri refused to clean up her internal dilemma herself, Lincoln acted swiftly and without debate, returning the entire state to Marshall Law and implementing emancipation, including the recruitment of black Missourians. Finally, well knowing that the Emancipation Proclamation was possible only because of the extraordinary powers given to the executive office during wartime, he committed himself to seeing the emancipation of the African-American written into the Constitution.

The President finally got the break he and the Union had been praying for. Within a few days of each other, the victory of Union forces at Gettysburg and Vicksburg sealed the certain demise of the Confederacy. In the days following, knowing that it was only a matter of time now, Lincoln began to reflect on the fundamental meaning of the Civil War. The fruit of his reflection was the Gettysburg Address which, in comparison with Lincoln's previous speeches, illustrates clearly the depth of his conversion and puts to rest any discussion of the causes of the war:

> *In invoking the Declaration now, Lincoln was reminding his listeners — and, beyond them, the thousands who would read his words — that theirs was a nation pledged not merely to constitutional liberty but to human equality. He did not have to mention slavery in his brief address to make the point that the Confederacy did not share these values. Instead, in language that evoked images of generation and birth . . . he stressed the role of the Declaration in the origins of the nation, which had been "conceived in Liberty" and "brought forth" by the attending Founding Fathers. Now the sacrifices of "the brave men, living and dead, who struggled here" on the battlefield at Gettysburg had renewed the power of the Declaration. "The last full measure of devotion" which they gave made it possible to "highly resolve that these dead shall not have died in vain" and to pledge "that this nation, under God, shall have a new birth of freedom."*[27]

---

27. Donald, *Lincoln*, p. 462

As is so often the case, critics often reveal an understanding of a man's words better than his supporters. This is particularly true of the backlash that followed the Gettysburg Address: ". . . Wilbur F. Storey of the ultra-Democratic Chicago Times recognized that by invoking the Declaration of Independence Lincoln was announcing a new objective in the war. Calling the Gettysburg address "a perversion of history so flagrant that the most extended charity cannot regard it as otherwise than willful," Storey insisted that the officers and men who gave their lives at Gettysburg died "to uphold this constitution, and the Union created by it," not to "dedicate the nation to 'the proposition that all men are created equal.' "[28]

But Lincoln was not alone in his conclusion about the ultimate nature of the Civil War. The nation affirmed his insight by giving him an overwhelming victory in the next presidential election. No president since Andrew Jackson had been elected for a second term. His success represented not only his own popularity, but the approval of the nation on the Emancipation Proclamation and his plans for reconstruction.

Lincoln's long apprenticeship was over. He was finally the leader that the nation had longed for and needed: "Lincoln had every right to be pleased with himself. After four exhausting years he was now fully master of the almost impossible job to which he had been elected . . . He headed an administration, and a bureaucracy, that followed his leadership. As party leader, he commanded overwhelming support in both houses of Congress. He was commander-in-chief of the largest military and naval forces the country had ever raised, and at last they were functioning with machinelike efficiency."[29]

The pursuit of justice gained momentum in the President as he looked to the future of the Union. His boldness caused even those

---

28. Donald, *Lincoln*, pp. 465-466
29. Donald, *Lincoln*, p. 575

closest to him to wonder. In place of recriminations and revenge, he looked to the full reconciliation of the Southern states with the Union. Soon after the fall of Richmond, he took the risk of travelling to the former capital of the Confederacy. He was surprised at the greeting he received:

> Landing without notice or fanfare, the President was first recognized by some black workmen. Their leader, a man about sixty, dropped his spade and rushed forward, exclaiming, "Bless the Lord, there is the great Messiah! . . . Glory, Hallelujah!" He and the others fell on their knees, trying to kiss the President's feet. "Don't kneel to me," Lincoln told them, embarrassed. "That is not right. You must kneel to God only, and thank him for the liberty you will hereafter enjoy." Quickly word of the President's arrival spread, and he was soon surrounded by throngs of blacks, who shouted, "Bless the Lord, Father Abraham's Come."[30]

With typical magnanimity, upon his departure from Richmond, Lincoln asked the surprised band director to play Dixie. "That tune is now Federal property," he announced, and it's "good to show the rebels that, with us in power, they will be free to hear it again."[31]

He returned from Richmond with a new sense of urgency about reconstruction. He now had firsthand knowledge of the devastation wrought by the war and a fuller understanding of the suffering it had caused soldiers and civilians in the South. More strongly than ever he felt that immediate action must be taken to restore stability in the conquered region. But few were willing to follow Lincoln's lead on lenient reconstruction. "He did not share the Conservatives' desire to put the section back into the hands of

---

30. Donald, *Lincoln*, p. 576
31. Donald, *Lincoln*, pp. 580

the planters and businessmen who had dominated the South before the war, but he did not adopt the Radicals' belief that the only true Unionists in the South were African-Americans."[32]

On the night of April 11, Lincoln appeared in Washington before an exuberant crowd celebrating the surrender of Lee at Appomattox. He made clear his plan for a reconstruction without accusation or recrimination. Finding again that middle position which would allow a "righteous and speedy peace" he showed himself in neither of the popular camps of the moment. In an astounding concession to the radicals, however, he acknowledged that the right of suffrage should belong to certain African-Americans, "the very intelligent, and on those who serve our cause as soldiers."

We began this chapter with a reflection on the term "conversion." Usually, the term is positive in its connotations, but as Lincoln spoke that night, someone in his audience had another kind of conversion — a dark conversion. In the heart of John Wilkes Booth, months of dreaming crystallized into a decision. As he heard the President recommend suffrage for blacks he turned to his companion and said, "That is the last speech he will ever make."[33]

Booth and Lincoln had many things in common. They were both physically strong, both famous storytellers, both urbane in their manners. They both had a passionate desire to make their mark on the world. But their hearts were made of different stuff. Booth was an actor whose heroic moments were more fiction than fact. Lincoln, on the other hand, knew the true meaning of courage and fortitude. Booth saw himself as a romantic hero of a fallen Confederacy. He decided "Our cause being almost lost, something decisive and great must be done."[34] How little the young man understood the meaning of those words, "decisive and great." On

---

32. Donald, *Lincoln*, p. 583
33. Donald, *Lincoln*, p. 588
34. Donald, *Lincoln*, p. 596

April 14, Good Friday, John Wilkes Booth assassinated a man whose life had been a paradigm of greatness.

David Herbert Donald chose to put this quote from Lincoln after the title page of his book: "I claim not to have controlled events, but confess plainly that events have controlled me." Yet, if nothing else emerges from *Lincoln* it is the personality of a man certainly brought to the forefront by dramatic events, but in no wise helplessly borne about by them. Perhaps the remark should merely be attributed to Lincoln's famous humility. Clearly, Lincoln entered into a dialogue with events. The shape he took as a man and a leader was the result of noble deeds directed by a conscience freed from the incredible bonds of political force.

In the moment following Lincoln's last breath, Secretary of State Stanton paid homage to the transcendent nature of Lincoln's actions: "Now he belongs to the ages."

The Pain of Patience

Few things are as frustrating as seeing human suffering without being able to do anything about it. Perhaps you have had the experience of watching a loved one endure the torments of a terminal disease — cancer, or AIDS, for instance. If so, then you know the silent agony of heart of which I speak, the helplessness and the frustration of standing before events you cannot control and riddles you cannot solve. You have experienced the search for comforting words, the desperate little gestures to ease the pain, the hopes placed on the so-called experts who come and go. And what if, in the midst of all this, you should discover that a cure existed, that your loved one's suffering was not necessary, but out of human error or malice such an antidote was unavailable or beyond your reach? What then? Wouldn't your silent suffering burst forth in a rage of protest?

Just this kind of feeling motivates those engaged in the battle for human rights. Once touched by the suffering of another, these people cannot look the other way anymore then they could ignore the cries of their own child, spouse, or parent. They know the meaning of John Donne's famous phrase, "No man is an island." Such was the motivation for the abolitionists who could not look at the South's "peculiar institution" as a matter of property rights — a merely political issue. They felt the pain of their brothers and sisters in chains, and the added pain of knowing that such a thing did not have to be. Such is the pain of committed pro-life Americans who grieve with every baby ripped to pieces in the womb, and every mother whose life will forever be haunted by the deed. Their suffering, too, is compounded by the knowledge that this horrible practice does not have to be.

The word "patience" comes from the Latin *patior* meaning to bear, to suffer, or to experience.[35] Patience is not just a matter of time or "sitting out" a situation. It has nothing in common with

---

35. *Oxford Latin Dictionary*, ed. P.G. W. Glare (New York: (Oxford University Press, 1983)

indifference or insensitivity to misfortune. On the contrary, patience always implies personal involvement. While it may have passive undertones – that one is subject to something and must carry something – patience is fundamentally active because it is a total response of the intellect and will of the person. As a virtue, patience refers to the willingness and ability to endure hardship or suffering. It enables us to bear suffering courageously and without rancor over a long period of time. Thus, implicit to patience are the virtues of faith and hope. We patiently bear a suffering in the confidence and hope that we will see its fruit.

In this chapter and the next I wish to offer a reflection on the patience of the two greatest movements for human rights in our nation's history: abolition and pro-life. I wish to show that compassion and human solidarity, coupled with a heroic patience, brought about the triumph of justice in our Civil War, and that these same virtues are at work now in defense of the unborn. In addition, we will consider the patience of a president who stood firmly for the right while at the same time knowing how to steer the nation on a steady course between two violent extremes.

Crimes that Scream to Heaven

At a distance of 135 years, it may be difficult for us to share the pain and indignation that motivated the abolitionists to the long exercise of patience that brought about emancipation. In this area, we owe a debt to historians and filmmakers who help keep fresh our collective memory. An example of powerful, conscience-moving story telling was Steven Speilberg's brilliant production of *Amistad*. Following closely the historical data on the slave trade, Speilberg opened a window on the past for us, setting before our eyes in detail the actual practice of the time. It is a difficult movie to watch, and I doubt anyone can ever look at African-Americans again in the same way after having seen it. Perhaps someday a great artist will lend his efforts to such a telling of abortion's bloody legacy. We need to be reminded — in words that come from the Nuremberg trials — "Lest we forget."

In case your study of slavery has been restricted to the cold climate of academia, with all the emphasis on memorizing the facts and no allowance made for the vibrating chords of human sympathy, I offer you now a brief description.

The story of slavery did not begin with some white-skinned, foreign invader. On the contrary, Africans betrayed Africans.[36] They sold one another to white slave traders in exchange for gold, iron, beads, copperware, brassware, alcohol, and guns. Nor should we assume that the Africans who perpetrated this crime were a barbarous, ignorant people. At the time that the slave trade began, roughly 1400, West Africa was a flourishing culture. The African nations were fully civilized societies with powerful armies, organized governments, productive economies, systems of law and education, and skilled artisans. Greed, not ignorance, moved Africans to sell other Africans to the white man.

At first, coastal tribes sold slaves from their own regions, but as the demand increased it was necessary for captives to be taken from the interior and uplands. These were tied together with leather thongs around their necks in groups of thirty to forty, about a yard apart, and forced to march to the coast. The trip could take weeks. Many would die along the way from undernourishment or the unfamiliar diseases of the coastal region. Once at the pick up point, the captives were forced into overcrowded barracks where they waited an indefinite amount of time for the slave traders to arrive. Those who survived the march and the malnutrition of the barracks were then paraded like livestock before the traders. They were rubbed down with oil and poked and prodded to show off their finer points. Those who had no buyer were beaten, killed, or assigned to local household service. Chosen slaves were branded with a hot iron to identify their owners. They were chained together

---

36. Michael L. Levine, *African Americans and Civil Rights from 1619 to the Present*, Social Issues in American History Series (Phoenix, AZ: The Oryx Press, 1996), chapters 1-4

in pairs at the wrist and ankle and had their heads shaved; then, naked, they were rowed out to the slave ships.

The ocean voyage was known as the Middle Passage. The men were placed in the hold of the ship. On average, they had only a 6-foot by 16-inch area to occupy. In a hold of some height, one or two platforms could be added to increase the number of slaves. This meant that a slave lying in his space had as little as two feet above him. Hair and nails were trimmed regularly to keep the slaves from hurting each other in their desperate search for more space. In stormy weather, the ventilation ports were closed to keep out rough seas, making the hold suffocatingly hot. Sometimes, the women and children were placed in cabins and allowed to roam on deck; frequently, however, they also shared the hold.

The crew had good sport with the slaves. Women were fair game for sexual abuse. Those who resisted were beaten to death. In good weather, when the slaves were brought on deck, they were made to dance, notwithstanding the metal shackles that cut into their ankles. Those who refused to dance were lashed. Most slaves lived in fear that the white men were cannibals and they were being taken somewhere to be eaten.

During the 1500's and 1600's around 25 percent of the slaves died during the Middle Passage. At that time, ships were slower and voyages could last anywhere from forty days to four months. Traders often miscalculated the amount of food necessary. To ensure sufficient rations for the healthy, sick and dying slaves were simply thrown overboard. During the 1700's the mortality rate dropped to around 10-15 percent and there was some improvement in ship accommodations and medical care. By the 19th century, the death rate fell to around 5 percent. Of the approximately 12 million Africans taken as slaves from the continent, it is estimated that 1.5 million died before arrival. The figure is probably higher since there are no records for those who died on the march or in the barracks awaiting pick up.

Sale of the slaves took several forms. Sometimes a shipload had already been purchased and no other sale was necessary. Upon arrival, the slaves were simply delivered to the buyer. Sometimes the captain gave the slaves to a middleman who earned a commission for each slave he sold. Another way was by auction. On other occasions, a standard price was fixed for the slaves who were then brought out on deck before a waiting audience of buyers. At the sound of a gun, the buyers charged onto the deck towards the terrified slaves to claim the ones they wanted.

Once "home," slaves were gradually inducted into plantation labor. Slave children were sent into the fields well before adolescence, as early as five or six years old; by ten or twelve they were experienced field hands. Women worked side by side with the men in the fields. Pregnant slaves or slaves too old to work in the fields were given other tasks. Work lasted from sun up to sun down, as long as seventeen hours during certain seasons.

Most slaves lived in small wooden shacks, about fifteen-foot square, made of roughly cut and poorly fitted clapboard. These were cold in winter, hot in summer, and leaky in rain. Slaves had little or no privacy and they could be sold at any time. While they were allowed to marry, such marriages did not guarantee the couple would stay together. Vows were adapted: until death or sale do us part. Families were regularly split up. Punishment for rebellion or attempted escape was severe. Slaves had no legal standing and could not testify against a white man. They had no recourse and no appeal in any matter concerning their well being.

For a short while in our nation's history, slavery was restricted and seemed to be headed towards eventual and inevitable extinction. European countries were already ahead of the United States in their emancipation policies and criminalization of the slave trade. Greed reversed this trend in our own country. Eli Whitney's cotton gin opened up untold opportunities for wealth in the South's cotton industry, while slavery continued to be the backbone of the workforce. The new technology, coupled with unpaid labor, meant enormous gains for Southern plantation owners who were able to use their profits to build a unique culture, a way of life that they were willing to defend.

Perhaps this information reads simply as history for us. Perhaps the complacency of many years' distance and the knowledge that all of this has been taken care of in our laws keeps us from feeling the heavy price that so many African-Americans paid for the founding of this country. Is it any wonder, then, with the collective memory of our nation so dulled to the horrors of slavery, that abortion has been able to steal upon us unawares? A wise scholar once noted that those who fail to learn from history are doomed to repeat it. We are witnessing the truth of this dictum in our own time. The above reflection should help us see the immaturity of a political campaign run on the popular phrase "It's the economy stupid."

I shudder to think how many will be offended by the comparison I am making. They will indignantly respond that slavery and abortion have nothing in common and that I am somehow offending African-Americans by my insensitivity to their history. Such a remark, however, only reveals the moral blindness into which we have fallen and the need to see clearly what takes place in an abortion. I am confident that any human being of good will and open mind who allows this information to pass into his or her heart will understand the persistence of the pro-life cause and feel personally engaged to do something to help.

Even if we could argue that at the time of *Roe v. Wade* in 1973 most of the world was ignorant of fetal life, we can do so no longer. We know what lies in the womb; we know what abortion does to unborn human beings. One does not need a lot of rhetoric. A simple medical description of abortion is enough to cause a chill.

At present, there are several methods of abortion.

In the first trimester (the first three months of pregnancy) the most common type of abortion is suction curettage, *also known as* vacuum aspiration, *in which the unborn child is removed from the womb by a suction machine. The uterus is then scraped clean with surgical instruments called curettes. Another method is to use drugs to induce an abortion by blocking the action of the hormone progesterone in the woman's body.*

Second trimester abortions are usually D and E, *dilation and evacuation. The fetus is sliced up in the uterus and then removed. Medical personnel must scan the gathered body parts to insure that nothing of the unborn child has been left inside the mother. In another abortion procedure, saline solution added to the amniotic fluid that surrounds the baby burns his or her skin, mouth, and throat. The woman's body then rejects the dead child. Second trimester abortions can also be induced by hormone-like drugs called prostaglandins. These are added to the amniotic fluid causing muscle contractions that will expel the premature child. Those who for some reason survive these procedures are put aside to gasp out their lives — if not killed directly by the attending abortionist who may snap their necks or smother them.*

Partial birth abortion refers to abortions done during the fifth and sixth months of pregnancy and sometimes later. In this procedure the abortionist forcibly turns the child in the womb into the breech position and then pulls the living child by the leg out of the mother until only the head is left in the birth canal. The abortionist then forces scissors into the base of the child's skull, inserts a catheter, and sucks out the child's brain with a vacuum. He finishes his job by pulling the dead baby the rest of the way out of the mother. Though the American

Medical Association has asserted that this practice is never *medically necessary for the life of the mother, it is performed thousands of times a year in the United States. President Clinton has twice vetoed attempts to ban this practice. When Mr. Clinton told us, "I feel your pain," he certainly did not extend his compassion to the unborn.*

For pain is exactly what the unborn child feels. Consider this: by eight weeks old an unborn child has all the anatomy necessary to experience pain. By this age the neuro-anatomic structures are present, that is, a sensory nerve which sends a message to the thalamus, which then sends a message back to pull away from the hurt. If you stick a pin in the hand of an 8-week-old human fetus, he opens his mouth and pulls his hand away. He feels. Can we not feel with him?

And if this information is not difficult enough, how can we accept with indifference the knowledge that the perpetrator of this crime is the child's own mother and her partner? What can we say for her? Either she is gravely misinformed, desperately confused, or truly indifferent to the pain of her child or the promise of the life she carries within her.

Given all of this, can we begin to understand the kind of patient suffering that supports the efforts of pro-lifers? Can we drop the "fanatics" label for a moment — so carefully constructed by the media — and share with them the pain of watching the needless, violent death of so many innocent little ones?

I am not referring here to a vague kind of emotional tie with the unborn child. This is not on the level of animal rights. And although one may speak of rights in the legal arena, every pro-lifer knows that the concept of right barely touches the surface of the issue. The word "right" still hovers over the decisions of courts and legislatures as if life were a gift bestowed by a benevolent government. I refer to a heightened sense of the humanity of the

unborn and a profound realization of the meaning of human life —
its unique, unrepeatable, and precious reality.

In the last few years, pro-lifers themselves have realized that
their argument transcends politics. It extends to the value of life
itself. I mentioned in the introduction a cultural fascination with
"community." Pro-lifers are the boldest of the bold in their defense
of the human community and the reality of legalized abortion is for
them the pain of a mother losing her son, over and over again. In
recent years, we have seen even among pro-lifers a sharpening of
focus, and though their work necessitates legal and political
involvement, they are growing ever more aware of their status as
representatives of life in what John Paul II has called a "culture of
death."

We can see this culture of death playing itself out in the
women who have submitted to induced abortion. While slavery
was a great crime against humanity, each act of enslavement
involved one individual. With legalized abortion, each abortion
means two victims: the baby who dies, and the mother whose life
will never be the same again.

With the experience of twenty-seven years of legalized abortion
now under our belts, we are seeing the long-term effects of abortion
on the lives of women. A new term has been coined to describe this
illness: PASS (Post-Abortion Stress Syndrome).[37] This malady is
very similar to the stress syndromes discovered in soldiers who have
seen combat. It involves the repression of a memory of some kind of
traumatic, violent experience which has overwhelmed a person's
normal defense mechanisms resulting in intense fear and feelings of
helplessness – of being trapped and out of control.

Concretely, PASS means that women suffer recurrent
memories of their abortion or their aborted child. They may have

---

37. The information given here on Post-Abortion Stress Syndrome is
taken from the website article "A List of Major Psychological
Sequelae of Abortion" compiled by David C. Reardon, Ph.d,
copyright 1997 Elliot Institute, www.afterabortion

flashbacks of the experience and nightmares about the abortion or the child. On anniversaries of their abortion they may experience intense grief and depression. On the other hand, they may have the complete opposite reaction: an inability to recall the abortion; withdrawal from relationships, particularly with men; estrangement from those involved in the abortion decision; avoidance of children; a diminished interest in previously enjoyed activities; a rise in drug and alcohol abuse. Their personal relationships suffer as well: increased depression and violent behavior result in child abuse or neglect and a greater likelihood of divorce. And one abortion leads to another.

If we cannot feel for the baby we do not see, can we at least feel for the woman whom we do see? Given this information, are we not moved to protect her from herself? She is deceived when she believes that abortion is merely a matter of personal choice or that the life within her is just a bunch of meaningless cells. Those who purport to look out for her best interests have betrayed her. She is desperately alone.

A Selective Sympathy

Another echo from the past can be found in the political rhetoric surrounding abortion. The South consistently refused to speak honestly about slavery, calling it "our institutions" instead. Similarly, pro-abortion forces cloak the ugly reality of abortion with the term "a woman's right." Such word games are used to place the emotional energy of a people behind a project. Confederate rhetoric helped to enflame Southerners with the notion that the North was trampling on their rights — thus keeping attention away from the heinous nature of slavery. Abortion rhetoric does the same, subtly shifting public sentiment into one channel where we feel for the pregnant woman while remaining practically unconscious of the unborn life within her.

It is curious how a careful selection has taken place in the historical record of human suffering. We are encouraged to feel the suffering of some, but not others. We are often reminded, for example, of the seven million Jews who died at the hands of the Nazis, but seldom do we hear of the over twenty million Russians, the great number of Slavs, Christians, religious and priests, and the cruel treatment afforded to the mentally handicapped and the aged. Sympathy is energetically collected for homosexuals facing homophobia, discrimination, or AIDS. But, oddly enough, little sympathy is garnered for those suffering discrimination for religion. An astounding statistic appeared last year: hate crimes based on religion are second to racial hate crimes — even more so than the hate crimes motivated by sexual orientation.[38] When gays are victimized it qualifies as national news; but how often do we read of vandalized churches on the front page?

I am not diminishing the very real suffering of these representative groups. I am only saying that somehow it has become fashionable to suffer with some, and not others. It is fashionable to wear a ribbon in support of AIDS research, but "fanatical" to wear the little pewter feet of a ten-week old unborn child.

The sympathy selection process is particularly poignant in the right to life battle. In a story that clearly implies two protagonists, the woman suffering an undesirable pregnancy is always the focus of sympathy in the media while the child is a non-entity. We are told that without the blessing of *Roe v. Wade*, this poor woman would be forced to seek a life-threatening backstreet abortion. She has been rescued from her plight by the good, sensitive people of the Supreme Court who feel for her.

It takes very little to see that the scale is grossly imbalanced. Is no thought to be given to the baby ripped apart or burned to death in his mother's womb? Is there to be no human feeling for the half-born child whose brains will be sucked out by the attending

---

38. FBI Annual Report on Hate Crimes, November 1999

abortionist? Do we not sense that somehow our "compassion" has been perverted? The suffering of an unwanted pregnancy is not equal to the butchering of a baby. Nevertheless, in abortion debates the suffering of the mother is the focus, while anyone who would interject the suffering of the child is castigated as unfeeling and insensitive to the interests of women.

Of course, the central thrust of the suffering woman argument has been on a tailspin for years. With the gathering evidence on PASS (Post-Abortion Stress Syndrome) it turns out that abortion claims two victims, not one. The poor pregnant woman whose suffering was to end with a legalized abortion is, in fact, condemned to the worst imaginable physical and psychological torment over a lifetime. Women facing difficult pregnancies must be protected from a moment of fear and reactive thinking that may cause them to seek an abortion. We must offer these women other options than elaborate lies that will in time dissolve before the awful truth.

The process of perverting language and twisting human sympathy away from its true object is a *déjà vu* for this country. The South had no loss of words for its suffering at the hands of the North. They were being deprived unfairly of their property, of their "way of life," of their rights to self-governance. Many in the North, caught in the web of their own prejudice, had sympathy for the South's claims. "I am personally opposed to slavery" was a frequent refrain of politicians, while on the congressional floor they voted to maintain the South's property rights. This maddening contradiction between private and public morality was a constant puzzle for abolitionists and we find the same curious twist in moderate politicians today. There are many — even presidents — who have claimed to have pro-life convictions but seem strangely comfortable with the status quo of legalized abortion. "I cannot impose my morality," they say, as if an imposition of their convictions would gravely harm someone.

One way we can put our sympathies on the right road again is to meditate on the origins of abolition in this country. What was it that brought common, ordinary Americans of the 19th century into the unpopular cause of emancipation? How can we explain the fire that fueled their efforts and helped them resist ridicule and oppression? History written as a collection of minute details can dim the light of that first intimate and personal insight that made each new abolitionist realize he could no longer live as an island — that he had to stand and be counted for something no matter what his origin, age, gender or abilities. The content of that insight was nothing less than what the Founding Father's had hoped would be the basis of a new form of government: the worth and dignity of each individual human being and the protection of his or her fundamental rights.

And then, entering into that spirit that carried our nation towards a new birth of freedom, can we not understand what it is that has brought so many common, ordinary Americans of our own time into the pro-life battle? Is it not the same intuition on the value of human life? Is it not the same bond of solidarity with all human beings regardless of age, race, or creed, in the womb or out of the womb?

We must go further than the details of scholarship and reclaim the real content of our history. We must allow ourselves to feel again.

The Politics of Patience

In common speaking, patience refers more to the passage of time than feelings of compassion. A patient person knows how to wait. The old tale of the golden goose reminds us that we must be patient and accept the gradual arrival of our desires; otherwise, we risk losing what we already have. Other people can be angered or offended by our insistence in a matter they have not yet come to understand. Doors often close fast and firmly on those who try to push their way in.

Nowhere is this more important than in political life and the exercise of law. History has shown us that the victory of justice does not come quickly. The working of government takes time as it follows its necessary procedures while enlightenment proceeds slowly were cultural practice is strong. The pain of having to live open-eyed with injustice, of knowing that help is within reach but still far off, is augmented further by the long wait for society and the law to catch-up.

Abraham Lincoln knew the price of patience. He was constantly assailed for his restraint, especially by the people whose cause he embraced. Abolitionists were continually at work on him, pushing him to take radical action on slavery. He had made his personal opposition to slavery well known and his election to the presidency was greeted with great hope and expectation, much the way pro-lifers felt about Ronald Reagan and the hope of a human life amendment. But to win office, Lincoln had placed his personal beliefs aside and promised to protect slavery where it existed. He quickly demonstrated his intention to be faithful to his inaugural pledge. He also believed that to preserve the Union he had to steer a steady course between radical abolitionist demands and Southern interests.

For their part, abolitionists quickly realized that Lincoln was not going to bring about an immediate realization of their dreams. His political indecisiveness became a source of increasing frustration and they lashed out at him vehemently. They ridiculed and insulted him – their best friend in Washington! The great civil rights advocate Wendel Phillips labeled Lincoln, "that slave hound from Illinois," and Salmon Chase, Lincoln's abolitionist cabinet member, frequently called his boss, "foolish."

Yet, reviewing all that Lincoln accomplished — painstakingly leading the nation through a bloody war to a restoration of the Union and the emancipation of the slaves — I cannot help but ask the question, "Would he have been so successful had he not patiently tried to mediate between the abolitionists and the 'pro-choice conservatives' of the day?" I think not. Lincoln's crafty diplomacy and his willingness to work with the "racist Democrats" was the height of pragmatism in the best sense of that word. He saw slavery as an evil, and wanted to see the end of it, but he knew he had to go slowly. He was fond of saying the situation was like "a man who had an excrescence on the back of his neck, the removal of which in one operation, would result in the death of the patient, while 'tinkering it off by degrees' would preserve life."[39] Such patience paid off.

It is important to understand why Lincoln moved slowly on emancipation. This insight can help us accept and understand the slow evolution of pro-life goals.

Lincoln was a conservative man in the sense that he understood and respected the delicate balance at work in his society. He could see that the abolition of slavery would bring about a radical change and present challenges that, perhaps, the country was not ready to deal with. He had ample experience with the vehemence on both sides of the slavery question to know what would happen in the event of a sudden break. He understood that a resolution to an issue that generated such tension would not come in one quick action of law, as indeed it didn't, even following his Emancipation Proclamation. The caution with which he proceeded was, then, very understandable – and I want to emphasize the word "understandable" because understanding is the basis of patience.

---

39. Donald, *Lincoln*, p. 453

Though Lincoln took the opportunity to advance abolition, he kept a guard over his party, his officers, and his ministers lest anyone should leap ahead on emancipation before the time was right. Even after he decided for the Emancipation Proclamation, Lincoln waited for a Union victory. The Proclamation had to appear to be coming from Union strength, not weakness. It had to serve as a statement of principle and policy, not a whimper for foreign aid. Antietam was the battle that gave Lincoln just enough of a victory to move ahead with emancipation.

But even then, the emancipation he proposed lay only within his war powers as president and concerned only the slaves in rebel states. Lincoln knew how much to do and when. Knowing full well that once the war was over, so would be the effect of his proclamation, he immediately began the process which would bring about emancipation in the form of a Constitutional Amendment. The Emancipation Proclamation served as a kind of "half-way house" for a country long grown accustomed, not only to slavery, but also to the black man's low stature in society. Lincoln was not about to turn the whole thing upside down; rather, he wanted to allow it to work its way out naturally.

One of Lincoln's fears, which kept him from radical action, was the belief that freed slaves could not be assimilated into white society. For their sake, as well as domestic tranquility, he wanted to see them colonized back to Africa. He spent a lot of words and energy advancing this idea, even though right from the beginning, freed African-Americans themselves resisted it and maintained their rights as American citizens.

Lincoln's patience is attested to again in his final pleas to the South before the Emancipation Proclamation. In the fall of 1863, in a seemingly desperate attempt to avoid complete and official emancipation, Lincoln issued a kind of fatherly plea to the Southern states to give up the notion of being their own country. He issued them a promise saying if they would voluntarily elect to rejoin the Union through election of representatives who would take "their rightful seats in the U.S. Congress . . . they would be exempt from the final proclamation of emancipation."[40] Such a plan rested on Lincoln's two hopeless dreams. First, he figured many freed slaves would willingly leave the United States to form a new nation of their own in African colonies. Second, he figured the Southerners would voluntarily make the transfer from slave labor to the apprentice system popular in the North.

While we can respect the patience underlying this effort, Lincoln was straddling the border of "avoidance" strategy. One sees this kind of thinking in the belief of many moderate pro-lifers who would like to shy away from political action in the hopes that education will bring an end to abortion. Such an "education only" strategy relies solely on the voluntary cooperation of those who are doing the wrong thing to do the right thing. Lincoln hoped that slave owners would voluntarily give up their slaves, while "education only" pro-lifers hope that people will voluntarily stop having abortions once their minds are enlightened. Lincoln should have accepted the wisdom of his own words, "The Autocrat of all Russians will resign his crown, and proclaim his subjects free republicans sooner than will our American masters voluntarily give up their slaves."[41] If moderate pro-lifers saw the incredible similarity between their education approach and Lincoln's approach, there would be a great commitment to pro-life victories where they are truly needed, in the halls of Congress.

In the end, Lincoln realized that slavery did not admit of gradual solutions for the simple reason that there is no middle state between being a slave and being free. Even though he "let it be known that Union men in Missouri who are in favor of gradual emancipation represented his views better than those who are in favor of immediate emancipation," history proves he abandoned the former plan when he realized there is no such thing as gradual

---

40. Donald, *Lincoln*, p. 453
41. Donald, *Lincoln*, p. 453

emancipation. The courage to act on this insight made him our nation's most famous abolitionist and, more than any other American, the enduring symbol of abolitionist victory. Who can forget the image of Marian Anderson singing "My Country 'Tis of Thee" before the seated figure of Lincoln at the Lincoln Memorial? How many Civil Rights actions have begun and ended before that august monument?

Abortion, like slavery, is so huge a problem that it cannot simply be wiped away. Now, twenty-seven years after *Roe v. Wade*, abortion has wormed its way into our social fabric. We can borrow the term "peculiar institution" from history because that is just what legalized abortion has become among us. Supported by federal funds, taken for granted in the sex education of our youth, represented without emotion in evening television viewing — clearly, abortion has become part of the woodwork. As Sandra Day O'Connor noted in the 1992 Casey decision which reaffirmed *Roe v. Wade*, a whole generation has grown up since 1973 with the notion that abortion is guaranteed by a so-called "right to privacy" in the Constitution.

Yet, there is also no middle state between life and death. While pro-life activity must take the slow road of law and order, there will inevitably come the moment when a politician or a judge must face this fact. To paraphrase President Lincoln, every one of us must realize that we must annihilate abortion, or be ourselves annihilated. If there are compromises to be made, they must be in the areas of compassionate assistance to women in unwanted pregnancies. But on the question of the life and death of the unborn child, there is no middle ground.

Small Steps Before a Giant Leap

For anyone in the pro-life movement who thinks things may be too entrenched to change, consider the political scene as Lincoln found it when he first sought office.

In 1818, the territory of Missouri had applied for statehood and, in so doing, threatened to disrupt the balance of free to slave states (11/11) which had kept the slavery question comfortable and quiet. The North had gradually moved towards emancipation, while the South continued to build a culture whose economic support was slavery. Since Missouri depended on slave labor, Northerners were alarmed at the possibility of slavery's extension and the South's greater power in the legislature. Northern politicians proposed an amendment to the bill authorizing statehood, prohibiting the entry of slaves into Missouri and providing for a gradual emancipation of those already there. Since free states held a majority in the House of Representatives, the bill passed — but the slave holding majority in the Senate defeated it. The following year Maine — formerly part of Massachusetts — applied for statehood. Henry Clay spoke for the Southern states when he threatened that Maine would not be recognized if the restrictions on slavery proposed for Missouri were not removed. Senator Jesse B. Thomas of Illinois introduced a proviso by which slavery would be prohibited forever from Louisiana Purchase territories north of 36 degrees, 30 minutes. This, plus Clay's maneuvering to have Maine enter the Union as a free state and Missouri as a slave state, kept the antagonism at a standstill for the next three decades.

The name given to this political slight of hand was the Missouri Compromise of 1820. From the moment of its acceptance in Congress, wise men predicted that the issue of slavery was a sleeping giant. As other territories looked to join the Union the same question would emerge: would they be slave or free?

When Lincoln entered the political arena in 1834 as a representative to the House in Illinois, the country was just beginning to feel the surge of a new abolition movement. This time, the cause of emancipation was linked to religious conviction. Whereas the abolitionists of prior times had held to a moderate, gradual approach, these new freedom fighters held slavery to be a grave sin that could allow no toleration. They demanded immediate emancipation. Their publications had a militant, condemnatory tone that angered many and brought about violent responses. As we have seen, Lincoln did not appreciate the radical ideas of the abolitionists. Though he held that slavery was "founded on both injustice and bad policy" the promulgation of abolition doctrines tended "rather to increase than abate its evils." Respect for the law and the maintenance of good order were the young representative's first priority.

While Lincoln was busy building up his law practice and becoming an eminent figure in state politics, the country faced another crisis in regards to the expansion of slavery in the territories. War with Mexico in 1846 resulted in the acquisition of vast amounts of territory in the West and Southwest. Northerners supported the Wilmot Proviso introduced in Congress in 1846. It would have barred slavery from all the territories won from Mexico. The Proviso passed the house, but was defeated in the Senate. (Can the astute observer of politics of the '90's miss the haunting similarity to the defeat of partial birth abortion legislation in the Senate?) Southerners saw the Proviso as an example of a rising Northern control over national politics. Henry Clay once again proposed a solution. California, part of the land acquired from Mexico, would enter the Union as a free state — the rest was divided into New Mexico and Utah territories with no federal restrictions on slavery. The territories would have the right to exercise "home rule" in regards to slavery and decide for themselves. And the slave trade in the District of Columbia was outlawed. To put icing on the cake, the 1793 Fugitive Slave Act was replaced by the even stronger Fugitive Slave Act of 1850.[42]

The Compromise of 1850 was hardly a true compromise. A real compromise takes two opposing positions, each of which has positive elements, and creates a new policy which contains some benefits for each position. Whereas the Compromise of 1820 gave

---

42. The fugitive slave acts refer to the assistance that must be given by free states in the pursuit and return to the South of runaway slaves.

existing slaveholding states the right to keep slaves while forbidding new territories from establishing slavery, the Compromise of 1850 merely codified the nation's inability to take a definitive position on the issue.

In 1846 Lincoln was sent to the United States Congress as representative from Illinois. He voted for the Wilmot Proviso and other measures designed to confine the institution of slavery to the states where it already existed. He understood that some kind of compromise was needed and developed his own plan in 1849. The seeds of his greatness are found in this proposal which had two parts. First, the Federal government would pay "full cash value" if slave owners freed their slaves. Second, authorities would be required to provide "active and efficient means to arrest and deliver up to their owners all fugitive slaves escaping into said District."[43]

Lincoln's compromise of 1849 never made it to a vote in Congress. He angered Northern abolitionists like Daniel Gott who were aiming for immediate and total emancipation, but even more so Southerners like John Calhoun who wanted unconditional freedom to regulate the matter within their own borders. The fact that Lincoln's proposal failed in Congress only proves that Lincoln's sense of the weight of the pro-slavery forces was accurate. What is worth noting is that his effort shows him trying to move the country in a decisive direction, away from false compromises.

The Kansas-Nebraska Act of 1854 was the real catalyst for Lincoln's political rise on the issue of slavery. Most politicians had gleefully accepted Stephen Douglas's "popular sovereign" principle which allowed them to abdicate their responsibility as leaders and leave the whole issue in the hands of the people. They could wash their hands of the matter as easily as Pontius Pilate could over the death of the Lord. The decision not to decide and to turn authority over to the masses has always been the litmus test of

---

43. Donald, *Lincoln*, p. 136

cowardice in politicians. They may rest safely for the moment, but when the people have come to see the error of their ways, they know who have been their real heroes and who merely clever tacticians. To the one they will give the laurel of honor, while the other they will allow to drift into mediocrity. Lincoln's image can be found in nearly every city and town of our great nation. How often do we see the face of Douglas?

We have seen how President-elect Lincoln refused the compromises of Senator Crittenden's committee. As war became a reality, Lincoln was able to care less about pleasing the South and concentrate on taking small but decisive steps towards emancipation. The Confiscation Act, signed by Lincoln shortly after the battle of Bull Run, stated that a master would lose ownership of a slave if he employed that slave in any way to help the Confederate army. Even though the Confiscation Act was practically useless, it symbolized and helped bring about what the war would eventually guarantee: total emancipation. Moves like this were vital in keeping Lincoln and America on the right track towards abolition. If we could borrow a notion from the Catholic Catechism, such little laws have a kind of sacramental character because they bring about what they symbolize.

Little symbolic gestures sometimes annoy pro-lifers of the radical stamp. Some might criticize, for example, a bill that would force an abortionist to save the life of the unborn fetus. Where is the sense in that? Others may be irritated at the Knights of Columbus for putting up thousands of little white crosses for the unborn. What good does it do? These are obviously not major victories, but they are important small victories that should be encouraged and supported. They keep the country awake and moving in the right direction.

Masters of the Law

Law is a tool and, like all tools, its ultimate worth depends on the skill of the one using it. Good men who desire peaceful solutions to social problems have always had to be masters of the law and find ways within the law to correct injustice. This requires a deep love and respect for law as the means of social order. It also demands intelligent mastery of the law and the patience to follow due process. It sometimes even means letting the forces of injustice have their way for a time.

We can learn a lot about this matter from the life of Thomas More, Chancellor of England during the reign of Henry VIII. This honest man and able lawyer used every twist, turn and loophole in the law to defend himself from his enemies as he gave witness to the sanctity of the marriage covenant. Like Lincoln, More was a great lover of law. This love for the law enabled him to use it as the tool it is — for good. He also understood that even though law can be used in the hands of the self-interested and unscrupulous, law protects the individual by insuring as much as possible that each side of an issue must play fair. He knew his own safety depended on the King's strict adherence to his own laws.

Thomas More's story is beautifully told in the play, subsequently made into a film, *A Man for All Seasons*. In one scene, More shows his respect for law in a debate he has with his son-in-law. The younger man would overthrow all laws to pull down the tyrant Henry from his throne and save good men like his father-in-law from the gibbet. More's response to all this is a call to respect civil law, even if it protects wicked men. "I would give the devil himself the benefit of the law," he proclaims. "For what would we do after all the laws of the land have been cut down to get at the devil? Where would we hide when the winds of tyranny blow and they come after us?"

Abraham Lincoln stands beside More in his respect for the subtle details of law and his willingness to defend the law even when it served to promote something he did not like. Both More and Lincoln had a healthy respect for the evil of which men are capable. They both felt we should not upset the apple cart of law even if we see it being used to achieve ends we do not favor. This conception of law springs from a certain healthy self-doubt. One hesitates to destroy laws which one believes are wrong because one reasons, my beliefs might be wrong. In St. Thomas More and in the vintaged, mature Lincoln, we find coupled with this extreme reverence for law a sense of freedom towards it — the freedom of the seasoned lumberjack who can play with an otherwise heavy and deadly weapon because he knows he is the master of his tool.

An example of this mastery over law comes from perhaps the most unpopular move Lincoln made during the War. I speak of his suspension of the writ of habeas corpus. This, of course, meant that American citizens temporarily lost their rights to a fair and speedy trial. Federal officers were able to arrest, imprison, or even execute "enemies" at their own discretion.

The suspension of the writ of habeas corpus, though a military necessity, created an additional burden for the cause of abolition. It not only made an already unpopular war more unpopular, it gave those Northern voices who opposed fighting to free the slaves the advantage of being able to change the focus of their rhetoric. Neither the Southern politicians, nor the Northern "conservatives" liked to argue straight out for the goodness of slavery — any more than pro-choicers like to argue straight out for the goodness of abortion. Except for a few like Alexander Stephens, who actually extolled the virtues of being a slave, most Americans just wanted to keep slavery out of the whole debate. Once the writ of habeas corpus was suspended, they could argue against Lincoln without arguing for slavery. Those who were opposed to the war were able to turn their campaign into a call for law and order against a tyrant, and attribute to themselves a genuine love for the Constitution. This was a very crucial bit of political strategy used at peace rallies throughout the North.

It is important to understand the power of the Northern, anti-Lincoln position. It was popular because it seemed so right. The Constitution, it was thought, was the foundation upon which this country was built. Attack it and the country collapses. Lincoln was a victim of his own previously held position. His adversaries may have been intellectually blind to the humanity of the African-American, but they were clever and clear when it came to twisting the law. A bit of common wisdom warns that stupid enemies are not as great of a problem as smart ones.

In response to the vicious attacks he received, especially from Justice Taney of *Dred Scott* fame, Lincoln responded with one of the most intellectually fascinating remarks of the whole war: "Such extreme tenderness of the citizen's liberty," as Taney had shown, could lead to the danger of allowing "all the laws but one, to go unexecuted, and the government itself go to pieces, lest that one be violated."[44]

Do you see the incredible similarity between these words of Lincoln and St. Thomas's reference to a political tyranny that springs from the loss of the rule of law? The wisdom of this statement reveals the President's extraordinary statesmanship. It does not attack the major premise of Taney's argument; in fact, it assumes the validity of that premise. It is fundamental for society to follow the law. But instead of shooting from the hip, and saying something like, "I can't worry about law and order at a time like this," Lincoln actually raised the nation's expectations and appreciation for law and order. He forced America to contemplate a higher law to which the Constitution itself owed allegiance. Lincoln was using the same wisdom we find in the words of Christ when He said, "The Sabbath laws were made for man, not man for the Sabbath." As an honest and trusted lawyer, Lincoln obviously knew the importance of fair and just courtroom trials; but he also knew his enemies were not above hiding behind one piece of law while working furiously to dismantle another piece of higher law.

Patience kept Lincoln from stooping to the same level as his enemies. Maybe this response is difficult for us to understand these days. When I was a young boy, I learned a powerful lesson about

---

44. Donald, *Lincoln*, p. 304

justice from my comic books: good guys are supposed to bind themselves to obey the higher law of justice even when that obedience would place them at a disadvantage with the bad guys. Did you ever feel frustrated during those scenes when the Joker or the Penguin would hold Batman accountable for their just protection under the law? Even when they had been thwarted in their plan to send the Caped Crusader and Robin to a horrible death? How many times did Batman or Superman turn the tables on a villain, but stop just short of dropping him over a cliff or into a vat of boiling water? As a child, I hoped they would . . . but something told me it was right that they did not. We were taught that fidelity to a higher order was what made a hero a hero.

Unfortunately, in the modern remakes of these American classics, the villains are destroyed in the end. They usually meet their end by falling into the bottomless pit, or being vaporized or otherwise "offed." Such a pattern is now the standard in Hollywood, a subtle sign of our nation's distrust of the penal system. In the originals, after Batman or Superman had bagged the criminals, policemen — who were obviously less than superheroes — hauled the offenders away to jail. In days before September 11, ordinary police officers were rarely candidates for superhero status. They only represented the strict legalist, merely following orders, merely following the letter of law. Law has its sacred place in society, but it takes a superhero to master the law. Those who died in New York's World Trade Center became heroes because even the law of self-preservation was surpassed.

The suspension of habeas corpus may have looked like an extreme to the moderates, but Lincoln understood that the issue at stake was so important for the life and health of the nation that such measures were fully warranted. Thomas More had the same clarity of vision about Henry's desire to divorce and remarry. Perhaps he would not have gone to the extreme of resigning his office if the marriage in question had been of some unknown shoemaker; nor would the king have demanded his execution for treason if More had been simply the local blacksmith. But the actions of kings and their ministers cannot be ignored. They determine the conscience of a people. Thomas More knew he was giving up his life to save the king and the nation from the evil that would follow in the wake of divorce. Lincoln realized his own martyrdom everyday of his presidency and finally paid the ultimate price for his convictions.

When Americans stand in silence within the cold marble shrine of the Lincoln Monument, they do not remember with disdain Lincoln's suspension of the writ of habeas corpus. Most probably do not even realize that such a thing ever happened in this country. The reason we don't remember it is that a greater good, the freedom of African-Americans from slavery, has overshadowed whatever measures had to be taken at that time. But let us not forget that emancipation did not happen in one quick stroke of the pen. Nor will the end of legalized abortion happen so neatly. We must have patience. We must work within the law. We must be prepared to accept small steps and simple measures. At the same time, we must be ready — and our leaders must be ready — to walk in a single direction, and stop the fence sitting.

American Heritage

Partners in Crime

In many ways, slavery and abortion share a historical pattern of conception and growth. Both spread silently and steadily, fed by greed and prejudice. Both settled into everyday life on the same footing as any other business transaction. Both required the numbing of the nation's conscience and the invention of a special vocabulary to maintain their existence.

Slavery was in practice on the North American continent well before the time of the American Revolution. It spread geographically with colonization. In the late 18th and early 19th centuries, however, a movement to abolish slavery was underway in Britain and France. The United States soon followed suit. Early on, the Society of Friends, commonly known as the Quakers, provided an organized and effective voice against slavery in the colonies. They were joined by some of our nation's Founding Fathers, notably Benjamin Franklin, Alexander Hamilton, John Jay, Thomas Paine and Benjamin Rush. These men had no doubt that slavery represented a negation of the principles enunciated in the Declaration of Independence, but they also recognized that their infant nation was not ready for its abolition.

The abolition movement saw small but steady gains over the years. At first, it was a state to state battle. Vermont outlawed slavery in 1777, and Massachusetts found it to be inconsistent with its new state constitution of 1780. Other states took a gradual approach. Pennsylvania, New York and New Jersey passed laws freeing the children of slaves. By 1804 every state in the North had on the books some kind of emancipation law. In 1808, the United States withdrew permanently — at least officially — from the African slave trade. The South, too, advanced towards emancipation, having little reason to resist these measures. The harvesting of cotton was a slow, tedious process requiring hours of work by hand. Slavery was simply too expensive an institution to keep going under such conditions. It could even be said that by the end of the 18th century slavery in the United States was on the road to extinction.

But then the picture changed radically. Whatever progress the abolitionists had made came to an abrupt end with the invention of Eli Whitney's cotton gin in 1793. Suddenly, one slave working a cotton gin could do the work of a thousand. The South headed towards an economic boom. By 1860 the South had gone from a few thousand bales of cotton produced yearly to an astronomical four million bales yearly.[45] Along with the increase in cotton production came a greater demand for slaves. And so the formula went: more land — more slaves — more cotton.

For awhile, a hush seemed to fall over the South's activities, but territorial expansion and the need to define the nation's position on slavery caused a surprising awakening in the nation's citizens. Northern states had already taken decisive steps toward complete emancipation and expected their Southern neighbors to follow suit. This did not happen. The North began to realize that greed had quietly and insidiously strangled the South. The final result was not merely the institution of slavery, something the world had known since time immemorial, but a unique kind of slavery based not on conquest of a people, but on their skin color. This prejudice became the basis for Southern culture. When the Confederates spoke of defending their way of life, it was the preservation of this prejudice and its sustaining institutions that they meant. The evidence of this is to be found in the long history of civil rights work extending even into our day.

Abolition was a long and patient process. Working against a public steeped in prejudice and custom and, in the South, the economic factor, abolitionists were seen as fanatical. Many in positions of influence and power would automatically close their

---

45. *Historical Statistics of the United States*, quoted in The Civil War Project, www.germantown.k12,il.us/html/abolition.html

doors and ears to anyone with the taint of abolitionist involvement. In addition, since the North adopted abolitionist beliefs first, abolition became associated with a particular region and, consequently, a threat politically in the balance of legislative power. The crusade for human freedom became entwined and blurred with this regional power play — Northern interests vs. Southern interests. The South began to fear Northern domination and this, rather than the slavery question, began to move to the center of a national emergency.

Just as slavery wormed its way into American culture, abortion also crept in by a back door and took a squatter's position in the culture. The alleged constitutional "right to privacy" which the Burger Court used to justify legalized abortion had been carefully cultivated over the years. It made its first appearance with the relaxing of laws on pornography and contraception. This, plus the sexual revolution and the rise of a new feminism — radically departed from the goals of its founders — had carved into the social conscience a different set of standards for right and wrong. The ground for *Roe v. Wade* was carefully hoed and cultivated. Yet, in retrospect, though one can see the gradual and certain movement towards legalized abortion throughout the sixties, the 1973 Supreme Court decision in *Roe v. Wade* took most people by surprise.

The early seventies were a watershed time for American confidence in its political institutions. A long drawn out and unsuccessful conflict in Vietnam had created a "credibility gap" between the people and government officials. At the same time that the Supreme Court handed down their decision in *Roe v. Wade*, Richard Nixon was caught up in the Watergate scandal and the nation had its first real view of insider's politics. The wholesale betrayal of the nation's unborn children was part and parcel of a political spectrum gone mad.

Up to the Nixon era, Americans took for granted that their leaders for the most part were in pursuit of a just, ordered society.

Certainly, the country's history had its share of villains and idiots, but the core of American values was assumed to ride out the fluctuations of political history. As one woman put it, " . . . I remember that someone said they had seen something on TV about the move to legalize abortion. We never felt we were going to be involved . . . We thought our legislators would take care of it. But they didn't."[46] Resting in this complacent picture of a fundamentally good nation, most Americans did not see the gradual dimming of legal protection of the family and civil rights. In fact, a smoke screen of fervent rhetoric on civil rights seemed to hold out the promise that we were becoming a more just society at every turn.

The complacency of Americans before the *Roe v. Wade* decision has its parallels in the optimism that permeated this country in the mid-19th century. While storm clouds gradually collected on the horizon, most Americans were looking toward the future with great expectations. A wide, unsettled continent lay before them; land was plentiful and with hard work and a bit of luck the sky was the limit. One sees this great optimism, for example, in the paintings of the Hudson River School with their beautiful scenes of the American landscape, abundant harvests, and rosy cheeks on the faces of shoeless little children. An idyllic picture, for sure, augmented by the preaching of ministers who insisted that America was the new Promised Land and George Washington the new Moses.

But the reality of the nation's situation in the 1850's was not as Americans wanted to believe, anymore than it was in the 1960's before *Roe v. Wade*. The promise of prosperity belonged to some, not all, and certainly not to those in bondage. Nor did the dream come easy. The frontier was a cruel and unforgiving place and for

---

46. *New York Times*, 25 November 1978, 28, quoted in Abortion and American Politics, Barbara Hinkson Craig and David M. O'Brien (Chatham, New Jersey: Chatham House Publishers, Inc., 1993), p. 42

every family that found a new life on the frontier, there were others who found death and disease.

Pro-lifers are sometimes accused of being morose and not seeing the positive elements in modern culture. Many people are uncomfortable at the suggestion that underneath the boom of materialism we enjoy there are ugly realities such as abortion, fetal experimentation, assisted suicide, etc. We must not forget, however, no matter how the artists of our day paint for us lovely pictures of our society, that human life is marked by both suffering and joy, good and evil. Abortion clinics may have flowers planted along their walkways, but inside, death is for sale.

Taking on the Establishment

It is easy for us now to look with fondness and affection on the abolition movement that gained for our nation such a great good as freedom for all our citizens. It is easy to forget that in its time, abolition was not a popular cause, and its members received continual and dirty pummeling in the press. Even in the North they were denigrated and ridiculed. Few mainstream politicians were willing to be associated with the abolitionist cause, including Abraham Lincoln, the future hero of emancipation. Pro-lifers can rightly find consolation and encouragement in the sufferings of their forebears in equal rights.

In the twenty years that followed the Missouri Compromise, abolition efforts temporarily faded into the background as the nation breathed a sigh of relief. No new territories were added to disturb the balance in Washington, and conditions in the South had settled into a kind of comfortable permanence. Yet, the issue had not died. There were those who continued to stoke the fires of abolition all through the thirties. To silence them, the House of Representatives in 1836 established the so-called gag rule which automatically tabled every petition of an abolitionist nature before it could be sent to committee. John Quincy Adams led the opposition to such a blatant attack on civil rights. Abolitionists suffered another humiliation at the hands of Andrew Jackson and Martin Van Buren who maneuvered postmasters to stop delivering abolitionist literature to the South. It was clear to all that the South, to keep her precious institution of slavery, was willing to tread on the most sacred rights of the nation.

Abolitionists were frustrated at every turn on the political level. Then, in the 1830's the very nature of the movement changed. With the publication on January 1, 1831 of William Lloyd Garrison's *The Liberator*, abolition was wedded to a national religious revival and took on crusading force. Garrison wrote, "I do not wish to think, to speak, or write with moderation . . . I am in earnest — I will not equivocate — I will not excuse — I will not retreat a single inch — AND I WILL BE HEARD." In 1833, abolitionists joined together to form the AAS, American Anti-Slavery Society. Within two years they had a flourishing network of members throughout the states. They founded newspapers, held rallies, and distributed emancipation materials. By 1840 the AAS had 1,650 chapters and an estimated 130,000 to 170,000 members. Graphic descriptions of slave capture, slave ships, slave trade, and the daily reality of slavery were everywhere promulgated in the abolitionist press and in special handouts and posters. Frederick Douglass, Angelina Grimké, Wendell Phillips, and Theodore Weld were well known orators on the subject. Public education in the matter was assisted also by the publication in 1839 of Theodore Weld's American Slavery As It Is. In 1852, Harriet Beecher Stowe used material from Weld's book to write *Uncle Tom's Cabin*, the book that put the American abolitionist cause before the whole world.

A series of frustrating setbacks in the 1840's caused the abolitionist movement to break into fragments. Some wanted to extend their cause to include women's rights and prohibition. Some abolitionists eschewed high profile, political involvement and concentrated instead on the suffering individual. They were attentive to the actual condition of the blacks. They founded schools and libraries and provided safe haven for escaped slaves.

Few have not heard of the valiant efforts of Harriet Tubman and the Underground Railroad. The American Colonization Society advocated the return and colonization of Africans to their native continent.

Of particular importance in the story of the Civil War are those bills, resolutions and compromises that opened the door, little by little, to the grand entrance of the Emancipation Proclamation. We have already looked at one such step, the Confiscation Act of 1861. In the shadow of the Emancipation Proclamation, the value of these small victories seems rather insignificant. But, though they were far from the ideal, Lincoln and other anti-slavery politicians consistently used them for the eventual freedom of the slaves.

Some abolitionists felt what was needed was the formation of a real political party to take its place alongside the Democrats and Whigs. This became the Liberty Party which eventually evolved into the Free Soil party with the specific platform of opposing slavery in the territories acquired from Mexico. In 1848 the Free Soil party nominated Martin Van Buren, formerly the eighth president of the United States from 1837-1841 but lost that election to Zachary Taylor. Eventually, abolitionists and Free Soilers joined together with other interest groups to form the Republican Party. After failing to gain the presidency in 1856 with John C. Frémont, they succeeded in 1860 with Abraham Lincoln on a moderately abolitionist platform which gave firm opposition to the expansion of slavery into the territories while maintaining a policy of non-interference in the states where slavery already existed. Lincoln pledged himself to upholding this platform and did so until he was brought to the conclusion that slavery was the cause of disunion and had to be eradicated if the nation was to survive.

Unfortunately, some abolitionists turned to violence. John Brown led a Free Soil militia group in Kansas. In 1856 he responded to pro-slavery aggression by attacking and brutally killing five pro-slavery settlers in Lawrence, Kansas. Three years later he hoped to incite a slave insurrection by his attack on

Harper's Ferry, Virginia (now West Virginia). Federal forces under Robert E. Lee promptly recaptured the arsenal. Brown was convicted of treason against the state and hanged. His execution raised him to the rank of a martyr for the cause.

The greatest blow to abolition efforts came in 1857 with the Supreme Court's decision in *Dred Scott v. Sandford*. In one fell swoop the Court seemed to undo the work of a generation. On the contrary, *Dred Scott* became the rallying cry of a re-invigorated abolitionism and stands as an inspiration to the pro-life movement today. Clearly, the word of the Supreme Court is not final. Lincoln found such fault with the *Dred Scott* decision that he was able to extricate himself from a slavish devotion to law and discover the higher principles that guarantee judicial and legislative justice. *Roe v. Wade* has done the same thing for many Americans. It has made us stop and take stock of what we believe and what we expect from our laws. In a legal sense, we have had to grow up.

Pro-lifers can find a lot to relate to in the challenges and evolution of the abolition movement. To meditate on this history is to find consolation and encouragement in the battle to end legalized abortion.

For one thing, pro-lifers came first from among ordinary citizens, just as did the abolitionists. These words from Frederick Douglas describing the women who maintained the cause of abolition could very well describe many pro-lifers of our time:

> *[He] pointed to the "skill, industry, patience and perseverance" shown at "every trial hour," the willingness to "do the work which in large degree supplied the sinews of war," and the "deep moral convictions" that helped to give abolitionism its character. As Douglas knew, it was white middle-class and some black women who did much of the day-to-day work of reform. For more than three decades, they raised money, created and distributed propaganda, circulated and signed petitions, and*

lobbied legislators. During the 1840's and 1850's, they helped to keep the moral content of abolitionism alive when a diluted political form of antislavery emerged.[47]

One study of early pro-lifers revealed that they were "predominantly women homemakers without previous experience in political activities."[48] As with abolition, pro-lifers gradually gathered experience and political savvy — but at first, it was the "remnant" who carried the day.

Another parallel to abolition history is the role of religion. The abolition movement received new life and impetus from the spirit of religious revivalism that swept the United States in the early 19th century. Slavery was condemned on biblical/religious grounds and anyone who supported it was thought to be in league with the devil. In a similar way, *Roe v. Wade* came about just as "born again" evangelical Protestantism was making its presence felt. With abortion at the top of its list of reforms, the evangelical movement eventually became the backbone of pro-life activity.

While it is true that in the days following *Roe v. Wade* only the Catholic Church could provide some kind of organized response (just as the Quakers served as the first organized body of resistance to slavery in the 18th century), the media is seriously outdated when it labels abortion a "Catholic issue." Many other religious denominations and secular organizations have moved to the forefront of the movement. The horror of partial birth abortion even elicited a response from the usually pro-abortion American

---

47. Julie Roy Jeffrey, The Great Silent Army of Abolitionism, Ordinary Women in the Antislavery Movement (Chapel Hill and London: The University of North Carolina Press, 1998), p. 2
48. Kristin Luker, Abortion and the Politics of Motherhood (Berkeley: University of California Press, 1984), pp. 137-144, quoted in Abortion and American Politics, Barbara Hinkson Craig and David M. O'Brien (Chatham, New Jersey: Chatham House Publishers, Inc., 1993), p. 46

Medical Association. One can find on the internet, pro-life groups representing African Americans, feminists, atheists and agnostics; as well as professional organizations in the medical sciences and law. It may be convenient and easy to continue labeling the pro-life movement a Catholic effort, but the reality is this issue has cut across every field and religious and philosophical persuasion.

As for strategy, right to life efforts have followed a familiar pattern. Taking a cue from Abraham Lincoln and the moderates of the Civil War era, pro-lifers have attempted to restrict abortion — prevent its expansion, in other words — while working at the same time for a constitutional amendment protecting human life from conception to natural death. At first, right to life work took place on the state level, pushing the limits of the power to regulate abortion in the states which was loosely provided for in *Roe v. Wade*. Restricting state and federal funds, passing legislation mandating informed consent, and insuring the legal protection of the viable fetus could hold abortion in check. In addition, pro-lifers have tried again and again to bring the case in various guises before the Supreme Court, always hoping for a reversal of *Roe v. Wade*.

Just as the abolition movement suffered internal division over disagreements about strategy and scope in their efforts, so the pro-life movement has seen the development of different approaches to end abortion.

Some pro-lifers have come together to form new political parties with a specifically pro-life platform. Others have sought nomination as pro-life candidates within the Republican and Democratic parties, or urged the creation of pro-life platforms within these parties. Some have moved away from political activism towards the particular individual in need of help; Birthright, for example, seeks to help the pregnant woman resolve her difficulty without abortion. There are many in the pro-life movement who believe that the battle to end legalized abortion must be connected to other value-charged issues such as euthanasia and assisted suicide, pornography, and domestic violence. And, as at the time of abolition, there are those who cannot hold to the slow turning of the wheels of government. At times, their zeal for reform culminates in violence — the bombing of clinics and the shooting of abortion practitioners. On the other hand, many unborn lives have been saved and abortion clinics closed down by the peaceful, non-violent tactics of groups such as Operation Rescue or Pro-Life Action League.

The Legacy of a Just Cause

Strictly speaking, the work of abolition ended with the passage of the Thirteenth Amendment in December 1865 banning slavery. Its success was further solidified by the Fourteenth Amendment ratified in 1868. In the words of this amendment, no state could "deprive any person of life, liberty, or property, without due process of law; nor deny to any person . . . the equal protection of the laws." Finally, in 1870, the Fifteenth Amendment gave Northern as well as Southern African-Americans the right to vote. In addition to constitutional amendments, abolitionists saw to the passage of civil rights laws to protect the newly emancipated slaves. They raised funds to promote education programs in the former slave states and served there as reform-minded politicians, teachers, and ministers.

Abolition radically changed the political landscape of the United States. The echo of abolition was heard also in the rise of the women's rights movement. Women had discovered themselves politically in the abolition movement. They knew they could make a difference in society by uniting their efforts. Other social causes can trace their origins to abolition, for example, greater attention to the needs of the poor and the bitter effects of increasing industrialization, as well as improvements in medical care and education. Justice breeds justice.

Abolition brought together a truly democratic body of individuals representing many different walks of life, backgrounds, and viewpoints. There were some great ones in their midst:

Frederick Douglas, for example, whose intellectual and rhetorical gifts have seldom been equaled in American history, and Harriet Beecher Stowe who gave the movement an international justification with the writing of *Uncle Tom's Cabin* in 1859. For the most part, though, abolition consisted of quiet, unsung heroes involved in very ordinary means of public education and political persuasion. Wives and mothers worked, sometimes in secret, sending out mailings. They practiced a boycott of goods not produced in free areas. The democratic process was extended beyond the confines of legislative halls into the hands of the American people.

In the introduction we raised the question of "community." How is a society of so many different kinds of people to find a common basis for living together? The history of abolition provides evidence that human beings are truly capable of "community" when they are bound by principles. Such a divergent body of individuals found unity in their common opposition to moral evil. At the same time, diversity thrives when common moral standards are accepted. It is true that not all those opposed to slavery had the noblest of motives. Some opposed the institution because a free Southern workforce threatened wages and prices in the North. Others rode the crest of a popular movement to gain political prominence. But for the record, abolition ranks as one of history's great stories of moral fortitude and the triumph of the right. It gives us a clear path to follow to bring unity to our nation today.

Pro-lifers are on this path already. They are willing to take the heat for an unpopular cause whose time may not have come yet, but will. We can only look forward with radiant hope to history's judgement of the pro-life movement. Who will be our heroes? Whose monuments will stand in Washington? Which of so many stories will be immortalized on stage and screen? And, of course, the greatest reward of patience will be the living testament of countless Americans yet unborn. We are fighting for them.

Part II

The Trampled Vintage

What's in a Name?

Sociologists, psychologists and philosophers agree that human beings are social creatures. We congregate naturally and look to the group to understand ourselves. From childhood, we learn to size up our own situation in light of the common consensus. We are influenced by the majority opinion. If a certain boy or girl in class is popular, we instinctively want to be with them and like them. If a ride at an amusement park has a long line, we believe it must be a great ride; if a restaurant has a lot of cars parked in front of it, we accept that it must be a good restaurant. Within the Church such a spirit is found in a democratic search for "common ground." In the political arena, political labels reflect this social tendency because they make individuals easily recognizable as representative of a particular political philosophy or platform. They allow us to get behind one person or another during election time.

Many political purists would have us believe that banning labels from speech is the quickest path to political harmony. Though it is wise to realize no label captures all aspects of a public figure's personality, it is great sophistry to think that labels are meaningless. Believing that banning labels altogether as a way of stopping society's political struggles is a little like thinking that telling children to stop calling each other names on the playground is going to make friends of everyone. It certainly is a step towards preventing black eyes, but the "work" of making friends must involve an active pursuit of goods, not just a prohibition of evil. Dialogue is a necessity for the advancement of peace and social justice. Misunderstandings and misinterpretations may arise, but that is the risk we have to take. Would it be reasonable to expect the United Nations to be more successful if all speech were banned from their sessions? Maybe monks can find unity in the silent contemplation of the Triune God, but us normal people must be satisfied to work with the ups and downs of language.

Of all political labels, public servants are usually uncomfortable with the title "radical." They will scramble among themselves to be seen as someone who has taken the "moderate ground." One can easily understand this. In a republic, "radical" seems to contradict the nature of representative government whereas "moderate" suggests someone who listens to all sides of a question and accepts the will of the majority. Moderate implies popularity. It offers politicians the security blanket of "safety in numbers." The moderate is supposed to possess many positive characteristics: a calm, discerning, thoughtful disposition with no inclination to fly off the handle or become fanatical over something — a certain degree of stability. Such a one, so it is believed, never gets caught up in the whirlwind of change, but remains a steady, guiding hand. You can trust a moderate to keep things on an even keel.

We have seen how Abraham Lincoln rode to the White House on just this determination. He was able to placate the abolitionist North with his assurance of personal opposition to slavery, as well as the Southern Democrats with his guarantee not to interfere with existing slave laws. Of course, history teaches us that this moderate position wore thin in the end. By its very nature, a moderate position cannot result in the firm and decisive action necessary to resolve great conflicts. A moderate can be a good representative, but not a good leader.

A Rose By Any Other Name...

Let's put ourselves to the test. What label comes to mind for each of the expressions below: liberal, moderate, or conservative?

- reproductive rights

- open-minded, balanced perspective

- anti-abortion

Without spending $10,000 on a survey, I am willing to bet nearly everyone would agree that "reproductive rights" is associated with the liberal label, while "open-minded, balanced perspective" is paired with the moderate label, and "anti-abortion" is linked to the conservative label. We have been conditioned to grasp these associations.

For one thing, we need to recognize that while we use the terms liberal, moderate, and conservative pretty freely in our language, the truth is these terms are relative in nature and their meaning alters with the times. This fact explains an otherwise confusing aspect of the Civil War era. We are so conditioned by our contemporary understanding of the terms "radical" and "conservative" that studying the Civil War is bound to start our heads spinning if we do not develop sensitivity for the meaning of these words in their temporal context. For example, how would the contemporary media label a politician who said, "I don't care at all about the black man." Wouldn't he be considered a radical racist? Perhaps even a radical white supremacist? He would hardly be considered a moderate. What if a politician said, "I am for a black man against an alligator, but not when it comes to a black man against a white man." Another radical, extremist position, is it not? According to our labels. Yet, such were the words of Stephen Douglas and William Seward, two politicians of the Civil War period who were proud to be labeled "moderates."

How times have changed! In our day, do we not applaud the acceptance of other races? Even if in private one uses an occasional racial innuendo, a good American today would defend himself or herself by insisting the comment is only a joke, in the same vein that brothers and sisters of the same family may poke fun at each other with nicknames. It is important to appreciate this great accomplishment in modern American social thinking; that a negative label is attached to a racist mentality. This is not to say that we have entirely eradicated prejudice and racial discrimination. I only want to point out that we have come a long way since the days of Seward and Douglas.

What is hardly appreciated, however, is that such an incredible turn about in the American psyche is primarily a result of yesterday's radicals, not yesterday's conservatives or moderates. It is precisely because some Americans of the Civil War era endured the negative term "radical" that we can today boast of a more racially sensitive society. I say "endured" because one thing we can learn from radical-abolitionist Americans is that opponents use labels to achieve their goals. Sticking a label on someone can divert the public's attention away from realities and arguments. To be really successful politically, it is necessary to understand the fickle nature of political labels.

To illustrate this point, let's take another test. Who do you think this quote describes? "Many of the more conservative Republican representatives . . . were now lame ducks, and their influence was diminished."[49]

Could be a quote from NBC news about the latest situation on Capital Hill, couldn't it? In actuality, this is David Herbert Donald's description of Congress shortly before the 1864 elections. Donald continues: "They feared that Lincoln, after studying the election returns would fall under conservative influences."[50]

What kind of people do you imagine Donald is describing? Let me be more specific. In today's mind, are the people who are fearful of the "conservative influences" pro-life or pro-abortion? Since the pro-life agenda is generally thought to be a "conservative" cause, a loss of conservative influence would be a step back for it, would it not?

In the time of the Civil War, however, "conservative" had quite a different meaning from what we would expect. It meant wanting things to remain as they were. In other words, a conservative was certainly not an abolitionist. Abolitionists were

---

49. Donald, *Lincoln*, p. 395
50. Donald, *Lincoln*, p. 395

radicals. They wanted change. They wanted to stand the known world of values on its ear. They represented a threat to "business as usual." Few wanted to be associated with them and their "strange" ideas. Many were even afraid of them.

Who are the conservatives and the radicals of our day . . . really?

With twenty-nine years of legalized abortion under our belts, is it not the pro-abortion crowd who wants things to stay the same? Are they not dedicated to keeping abortion the status quo? Are they not continuing to apply the principles of *Roe v. Wade* to all areas of life? Yes, indeed. The pro-abortion contingent represents the preservation of a climate of radical individualism and selfishness that has eaten away the foundations of our social community. Now entrenched by custom and law, abortion serves as the watermark of efforts to maintain this culture of death. Its resistance to change parallels slavery in the Deep South of the antebellum years.

On the other hand, where do we see really radical thinking? Who has the gumption to suggest that life is a mystery? Who stands for life as a value in itself, independent of production or consumption? Who reminds us that every individual is unique and unrepeatable? Who has the guts to claim that the medical profession must be at the service of life not death? Who has called our judicial system on the floor for their disregard of the basic human liberty intended by our Founding Fathers? Who has blown the whistle on unscrupulous politicians who seek self-advancement at the price of the moral integrity our nation needs to survive?

Clearly, labeling pro-lifers as conservative is political incorrectness at its best.

A Step Backward or Forward?

"Progressive" has such positive connotations for us Americans. Isn't "American ingenuity" famous around the world? Do we not pride ourselves on being a people who can build the better mousetrap? Americans imagine the success of the American experiment is built on a break with tradition, particularly that tradition which distinguishes people into different classes. Many people believe that the more trappings of the past we can shed, the freer we will be to realize our greatness.

The other side of the coin, however, is that while most Americans enthusiastically applaud progress, they have given little thought to the destination towards which they are headed. "Time marches on" is a phrase many imagine means something truly significant.

Clearly, the term "progress" needs re-evaluating in our time. Who represents the really progressive element in our culture?

Moderate pro-lifers like to cling to the comfortable notion that they are the true progressives who are trying to bring change to society, but in the "right way." From their perspective they look down on radicals of either side and conclude that they themselves are holding the country together by keeping extremists from tearing each other apart. In reality, their effect in moving society in any direction is minimal.

The fact is, if we want progress, we must look to the "radicals."

At the dawn of the Third Millennium, we must realize that the previous century was the most homicidal in history. It began with a war whose dimensions and staggering death toll had never been seen before. We have witnessed not one holocaust, but many. The body count for transient ideologies mounted even into the last years of the century. Add to this the wholesale slaughter of unborn human life, sanctioned by law, the rise in euthanasia and assisted suicide, etc. Pope John Paul II was clearly on the mark when he described the modern world as a "culture of death."

To be pro-life means just that: *for life*. Pro-lifers have taken their stand on the value of human life from the moment of conception until natural death. They mean to build a culture of life in opposition to the prevailing culture of death. All of man's resources, all his science and skill, must be put at the service of life, not its destruction. This affirmation of life is so unknown in our time that we can speak of pro-lifers as today's "radicals." With a glance of pride back to our abolitionist predecessors, we can hope that our radical ideas will be tomorrow's conservative legacy.

For too long now pro-abortion ideologues have unfairly claimed to be the progressive thinkers in our society. For too long, they have marched under a banner of social change as though they were heroes and martyrs. One cannot help but think of the brave men in gray who went to defend the South's right to its peculiar institution. There is a tragic irony in courageous acts done for the wrong cause. We can be magnanimous and assume that most such warriors are simply ignorant of the facts — that their hearts are good, but their consciences severely deformed. When property rights are applied to human beings, when unborn babies can be murdered with impunity — no matter how glorious the defense of these evils, their proponents' honor should only be praised in the context of an invincible ignorance.

Pro-lifers must understand the greatness of their cause in this particular time and in this particular battle. They must refuse to be labeled conservative. That label has simply lost its meaning. One of the greatest lessons of the Civil War is that the disdained radical position of yesterday becomes the praiseworthy position of today. The radicals of Lincoln's time were leading the country. They were, as time would show, the ones Lincoln himself had to follow.

What Will the Newspapers Say?

Where are political labels born? In the media. Since labels can make or break a political career, no one who wants to see justice done in our society can ignore the power of the press.

Most of us ordinary Americans are fond of using the term "politician" in a derogatory sense. Since we are not famous and don't have to read about ourselves in the papers every day, we find it difficult to understand the pressure on a politician to maintain high public opinion. But politicians know they would pay a high price today for speaking out on behalf of the unborn. The penalty is swift and always the same. They are labeled "radicals" and "extremists," inevitably aligned with some kind of religious right wing movement, and whatever they have to say about any other issue fades into the sunset. The media wields such power over our public figures that they find themselves hesitant to speak in any but the most carefully chosen words. It is almost comical how politicians attempt to appear principled while really saying nothing.

For the most part, the media was brutal to Lincoln. Wilbur Storey of the *Chicago Times* described the Gettysburg Address as a "perversion of history so flagrant that the most extended charity cannot regard it as otherwise than willful despotism." He went on to write that those who died on the Gettysburg field "died to uphold the constitution, it had nothing to do with any dedication to the proposition that all mean are created equal."[51] If Lincoln had calculated his decision to free the slaves simply according to how the newspapers would treat him, he never would have signed the Emancipation Proclamation. The *Chicago Times*, for instance, denounced the Proclamation as "a monstrous usurpation, a criminal wrong, and an act of national suicide."[52]

One thing a study of the Civil War reveals is Lincoln's ability to give the media its proper weight. He highly respected the people's right to know what was going on and he knew how to enlist the media's service; but, above all, he knew when to ignore its power. He was a clever politician, and knew how to follow public opinion to the successful realization of his political goals; but he knew when to draw the line, as well. He was not the puppet of the press. America today must thank God that Lincoln did not

---

51. Donald, *Lincoln*, p. 466
52. Donald, *Lincoln*, p. 421

put more stock in making a name for himself than in being true to the inspirations of his soul.

Lincoln was also too wise to follow the up and down course of political editorials. Horace Greeley, for example, was one of the most powerful writers of the time. His articles in the *New York Tribune* were circulated throughout the nation. Lincoln understood that to disturb Greeley was to commit a great political blunder. Being the first to have "discovered" Lincoln on the national level, having given him a positive by-line regarding the Douglas debates, and further helping him along with a glowing review of his New York Cooper Union speech, Greeley certainly deserved Lincoln's gratitude. However, as the war dragged on, Greeley's power became more and more evident, while his political opinions more and more ambiguous. At first he praised the Emancipation Proclamation and even backed an abolitionist candidate for governor. When public support of the war effort began to ebb, however, Greeley vacillated, calling for a complete restoration of the Union "as it was" — meaning, with slavery — and suggesting that France or England be enlisted to negotiate a peace settlement. Yet, Greeley's fluctuations had no effect on the President. He remained firm in his convictions through the darkest hours of the war.

Lincoln also understood that the press had a responsibility to report the truth. One of the few times he allowed himself an explosive anger occurred following an act of deception by two gentlemen of the press. The editor of the *Brooklyn Daily Eagle*, Joseph Howard, and one of his reporters, Francis Mallison, took advantage of inside information about a possible new draft and printed a bogus story, reportedly from the White House, in which they greatly exaggerated the number of potential draftees. Just before the story appeared, however, they conveniently bought up lots of gold. Since draftees were allowed to pay someone else to serve in their place, thousands of men, in order to raise the necessary money, bought or sold gold, driving the price of gold way up.

The abortion industry – for that is what it is – presents us with the same kind of "profit by another's suffering." Every single doctor, nurse, or social worker who has left the "profession" has testified to the great "get rich quick" aspect of their "work." How we could use some Lincolnesque fury from the White House Today!

What Will the Relatives Say?

If Lincoln gives us a wonderful example of how we must give the media its proper weight, he also can teach us to rise above our fear of being ostracized by family and friends.

The Lincoln home was the scene of the same tensions at play in the rest of the country during the Civil War. Judah Benjamin, the Confederacy's Secretary of State, was one of the President's friends from his first days in Washington. Lincoln's brother-in-law, General Benjamin Helm (S), fought heroically at Murfreesburo in Tennessee and was killed at the battle of Chickamuaga. Quite a bit of controversy ensued when the General's wife Emile called on her half-sister Mary Todd Lincoln in Washington. General Sickles (N), who lost a leg at Gettysburg, told the Lincolns, "You should not have let that Rebel in your house." The President responded, "General Sickles, my wife and I are in the habit of choosing our own guests. We do not need from our friends either advice or assistance in the matter."[53] Great political differences should not prohibit common courtesy, but at the same time friendship and family ties should not overshadow the truth or weaken the fighting spirit that defends it. Lincoln was able to keep the balance between personal acts of kindness and the larger political issues at stake.

Nonetheless, the Civil War proves just how much the fight for justice can redefine fundamental, longstanding relationships. Just a few examples: General Jubal Early (S) defended the town of

---

53. Donald, *Lincoln*, p. 475

Fredericksburg as his old friend General John Sedgwick (N) led his men in a disastrous charge against the Confederates. Generals George Meade (N) and Robert E. Lee (S) had worked together as engineers before the war. General John Pemberton (S) surely must have known many childhood acquaintances among the besieging forces beneath Vicksburg since he had grown up in Pennsylvania. Admiral Farragut (N), who took New Orleans, must have had many in-laws who were staunch defenders of the Confederacy since both his wives were from Virginia. General Franklin Gardner (S), a New Yorker, faced two old classmates as he defended Port Hudson: General Christopher Augur (N) and General Ulysses S. Grant (N). General James Archer (S) had the unpleasant experience of meeting his old friend General Abner Doubleday (N) after he was captured by a member of the Irish brigade at Gettysburg. The list could go on and on. We may experience a strange mixture of shock and fascination as we remember such dramatic encounters. We cannot help but wonder what drove men like General Winfield Hancock (N) to such a point that he was willing to kill his old friend General Lewis Armistead (S) in battle. Fate be praised, such a tragedy was avoided as each man was killed within minutes of each other near the stone wall at Gettysburg.

Even more so than the broken bonds of friendship, the unnatural dissolution of family ties during the Civil War provides us with an insight into what ultimately unites human beings.

The old saying, "blood is thicker than milk" springs from the tragic situation of war, especially a civil war. The term "blood relative" usually means someone who is related to you by some birth order. However, where there is conflict regarding how life is lived beyond the nursery and fundamental issues of right and wrong are at stake, the bond between soldiers whose blood may run together on the battlefield becomes stronger than family ties. Mother's milk and father's seed bind brothers together under a family name; yet, a stranger who shares your ideals and dies on the field next to you, perhaps even saving your life, becomes a closer brother to you than your "milk brother" who is not on your side of the conflict.

Let us hope that our nation never again sees a war that turns blood relatives into enemies. At the same time, can we deny that even now within our families and among our friends we sense the presence of a divisive philosophy? The debate over abortion, unlike questions of taxation or education, has the power to turn a convivial gathering into a tense encounter between opposing ideologies. Whether in the backyard around the barbecue or during the coffee break at the office, raising the topic of abortion brings out an individual's deepest convictions about life. Just as with slavery, ambivalence is impossible.

The Civil War teaches us that human communities do not come together for convenience sake. They are a manifestation of shared values and commitment to a way of life. To say that man is social by nature means that he is capable of living a common life based on his understanding of what is good and true. When this understanding is clouded for some reason, all the ties that should bind and strengthen society are weakened and eventually fall apart. Secession and war rose out of the broken heart of a nation that had for too long endured the contradiction of justice for all and slavery for some. Call it grace, call it transcendent principles, or call it simply a light from above — what gives life to community is something beyond blood or shared circumstances. Whether on the large scale of nation states, or the simple relationships of hearth and home, what makes and keeps community is the love of truth and the pursuit of justice.

Though cherishing the ties of blood and friendship, pro-lifers have discovered their membership in a larger family than the one into which they were born. Many of them will tell you of how their lives changed after they became involved with the right to life movement; how they were presented with new experiences and new relationships that challenged them beyond themselves. The unifying power of truth gradually knit them together into a new people sharing a family resemblance of principle and self-sacrifice. They have received a new name in the blood fellowship that they share — the blood of the unborn children they have given their all to save.

Antagonists

Another philosophically charged word from the Civil War era is "antagonist." I am not referring to the simple meaning of the word, that the North was antagonistic toward the South and vice versa. I am referring to the term as it applied to two members of Lincoln's cabinet — one of the most troubled cabinets in presidential history.

David Herbert Donald refers to William Seward and Salmon Chase as "the two permanent antagonists in the cabinet." They were certainly extreme opposites on the question of slavery and both served as lightning rods for their contemporaries. Salmon Chase was so vocal in his opposition to slavery that when he offered his resignation Lincoln snatched it from his hands saying, "Now I have what I wanted." Lincoln, however, wanted the moderate Seward's resignation just as much. He had just about had enough of the division these two men were causing at the heart of his administration. Lincoln found himself the victim of his own desire to have a cabinet that represented both sides of the debate. It wasn't an easy way to run a government, but he did profit from the insights of both men and used their conflict to plot his strategy for the nation.

There were those who feared the influence of the brilliant Seward over Lincoln. "Old Abe is honest as the sun, and means to be true and faithful, but he is in the web of very cunning spiders and cannot work out if he would."[54] For all intents and purposes, it seemed that Seward had a real "in" with the president. Lincoln enjoyed his sense of humor and intelligence. Seward was a

---

54. Donald, *Lincoln*, p. 281

frequent guest at the White House for breakfasts, receptions and dinners. For his part, Seward believed he had Lincoln well in hand. His desire was to guide the President along the moderate path.

It came as quite a shock to Seward that Lincoln would name the abolitionist Chase to the cabinet. Seward took great pride in his moderate position and believed himself responsible for having saved the country thus far from war by giving in to the South on many issues. Chase, on the other hand, had no patience with the South's peculiar institution or its threats to secede. He looked for no compromise. Though Seward tried to get out of the cabinet rather than serve with Chase, Lincoln refused to allow him to go. Oil and vinegar were to be mixed together.

Lincoln had his share of difficulties with Salmon Chase. The Secretary of the Treasury was a sharp critic and political rival to the president. Chase was an ambitious man and he dreamed of occupying the White House. Lincoln's apparent apathy towards emancipation resulted in Chase's severest criticism. The secretary resigned three times — always as a political tactic. The third time, Lincoln called his bluff and accepted the resignation. Chase was stunned. At first he aligned himself with a short-lived group of Republicans opposing Lincoln's re-election. Later, he demurred and he and Lincoln were able to find a cordial footing with each other in Washington.

For all of their personal difficulties, though, at bottom Chase and Lincoln were of one heart and one mind about the importance of justice for the health of the nation. After the death of Roger Brooke Taney on October 12, 1864, Lincoln looked to Salmon Chase to replace him on the Supreme Court. Even though the President was better friends with Seward, he recognized the enduring value of the position held by Salmon Chase. He also knew that after the war the Court would be facing cases probing the strength and extent of emancipation. He needed someone with unmovable conviction in this matter to finish the work that he had begun with the Emancipation Proclamation. He showed his appreciation for Chase's moral courage by appointing him to the Supreme Court. Chase, the radical, received presidential recognition for his progressive thinking.

It's important to realize that although Lincoln and Seward shared the moderate platform for awhile, each man did so for different reasons. Seward could not see the sense of either side of the argument on slavery. He was not interested in the "just" answer. He simply wanted to avoid war, and was willing to do whatever it would take to maintain peace. Lincoln, on the other hand, though also trying to please both sides, always tempered his criticisms of the abolitionists by appealing to the practicality of their strategies, not the philosophical principles they held. If Lincoln sought balance in the diplomatic relations between North and South it was not simply to maintain a presumed ideal world in which extremists could live side by side undisturbed. Rather, he sought a balance between opposing sides with just enough of a tilt to move the situation forward towards true peace. As anyone who has ever ridden a bicycle knows, you have to be moving forward to keep your balance.

People who consider themselves moderates today on the abortion question would do well to reflect on the political career of William Seward. How many statues of him can you find in your area? How many roads and banks are named for him? Lincoln, on the other hand, is an American icon. Moderate pro-lifers must ask themselves if their kind of moderation is on the pattern of Seward or Lincoln. I once heard a Chicago priest state his views on the right to life battle very much in the keeping with the spirit of Seward. He described his frustration with radicals on both sides of the issue and maintained that the middle position would win in the end. But can such an attitude move this nation forward? If William Seward's plan had prevailed over Lincoln, is it likely the Union would have been victorious? After all, on numerous occasions Seward negotiated with the Confederacy for peace on their terms — that is to say, allowing slavery to continue.

Ironically, John Wilkes Booth included Seward in the assassination plot that killed Lincoln, probably because of the secretary's known friendship with the President. On the night of April 14, while the Lincoln's were watching a play at Ford Theater, Lewis Paine went to the Seward home where the secretary was recovering from a carriage accident. The assassin stabbed him repeatedly and left him for dead. Miraculously, Seward lived. If Booth had read the papers more carefully, he probably would not have marked Seward for assassination. He would have discovered that his pro-slavery ideology had a better friend in Seward than many others in Washington. He would have wanted him alive.

True Leadership and Representation

When all is said and done, the responsibility for the American Civil War rested on the shoulders of those politicians who refused over and over again to lead the nation towards a definite and just resolution of the slavery issue. The result: the madness of brothers killing brothers. Many Northerners did not want their "national brotherhood" to be broken apart, and yet were willing to kill their brothers rather than see them become citizens of another nation. Southerners were willing to lose their lives to protect their nice, "peaceful" way of life, which included enslaving other human beings. The inter-familial carnage of the Civil War stands now as an example of a nation's temporary insanity. What is essential for today is that we understand that this tragedy came about because the nation's leaders again and again put off the agonizing decision to take a stand.

My point is simple, but I believe now more than ever it needs to be brought into the light. When we say "representative" or "leader," what do we mean? One clear lesson from the Civil War is what happens to a society when elected officials define representation as placating the majority. True leaders do not simply represent their constituents, especially when the constituents themselves are locked in a stalemate. True, in a democratic, "tolerant" society it is difficult to call certain ideas "wrong"; but to realize something is difficult is not to say that it is unjust or should be avoided. When public servants refuse to make value judgements and allow themselves to be caught in the same stalemate that has gripped their constituents, they cease to be true leaders. By falsely assuming their purpose is simply to represent, they encourage rather than prevent the moral decline of their people.

In our own time, there are too many public servants who understand their job as just representing the crowd. They are quite right when they perceive that they may lose their position by being too radical or freeing themselves from the constraints of popular opinion. At the same time, they lose the heart and soul of their leadership position if they fail to move their constituents in some direction. I cannot emphasize enough this great lesson of the Civil War: yesterday's radicals are today's heroes. We do not need politicians who act as mouthpieces for the majority. We need leaders who are not afraid to assume a pedagogical position with their constituents — albeit with patience and understanding — but with clear purpose and direction.

Leadership is a unique and terrible position. While working with and among others, the leader is called upon first to raise his voice and cast his vote in controversial issues. Augustine, Bishop of Hippo, once said to his people, "I tremble when I think of what I am for you; I am consoled when I remember what I am with you." What he meant was that as bishop he had great responsibility to care for and protect the souls in his flock. He knew he would have to answer to God for the exercise of his office and this thought made him vigilant. But he knew his limitations as a man, too. He drew consolation from his status as a simple Christian, saved by the blood of Christ. In his humility, Augustine understood that he was one with his people, yet set apart. He knew the difference between leader and led. This knowledge enabled him to hold out firmly against the heresies of his time and defend his little flock from physical and moral invasion.

Abraham Lincoln was a man of this kind of humility. "Honest Abe" was very much of man of the people. He loved the telling of tales and jokes. He had lived at so many levels of society, from the poorest to the richest, that he could relate to a great many people. At the same time, he felt the weight of his office. One of the early actions of his presidency, which he regretted and never repeated, was allowing his bodyguards to sneak him into the capital for fear of a death threat. In retrospect, Lincoln decided that such an action was inconsistent with the role of president. Ever after, he refused to take extreme measures to guard his life, and made himself accessible a few hours out of every day to anyone who wanted to see him for any reason.

Lincoln also showed his awareness of his leadership position by the restraints he placed on his officers, cabinet and party. No decision about emancipation was to be made by anyone else. We have already seen how General Frémont was severely reprimanded for moving in advance of the President. Lincoln often frustrated his cabinet by not consulting them before a big decision. In retrospect, they realized that he did listen to them, and to a great many other people whom he felt could enlighten him on the various points of a question. He would strike up a friendly conversation with someone on a matter, never revealing that the whole time he was picking the other person's brain. His lawyer's skills came in handy. When Lincoln's biographers went to work analyzing his political style, they discovered a man who was truly open to all sides of an issue. He heard. But hearing alone is not leading. What made Lincoln great was that after listening, he decided.

What is an American?

In the history of the world, national pride has almost always been identical to racial heritage. A unique aspect of American nationality, however, is that our patriotism is distinguishable from race. Just as no one is born a Christian – he or she becomes one by acceptance of the Christian faith and baptism – so, too, when one becomes an American, there is in some analogous sense a kind of "conversion." By accepting the American creed, the naturalized citizen accepts the relative importance of his/her own ancestry and removes his birth-nationality from the pedestal that places it above all others.

What makes an American, therefore, is not blood or land, but fidelity to a set of ideals. This being the case, a great part of our history has revolved around the construction of a community of racially diverse, culturally sensitive citizens who yet share a common belief in human dignity and fundamental rights spelled out in the Declaration of Independence and the Constitution. This has not been an easy task, but the ties that bind Americans are strong because they are not merely ideological. America is not just another passing form of government. This ideal she represents of the relative importance of his/her own birth nationality flow from God and are engraved on human nature. If the South lost the Civil War, it was because ultimately she did not represent America's truest ideals. With the North's victory, the United States was able to retrace its steps to its noble origins and begin again. It meant, as Lincoln called it, "a new birth of freedom" for our country and a clearer definition for each American of what it means to bear that name.

We can derive from this reflection a greater understanding of what brought about the Civil War and why the North's victory is so important. When one's natural love and loyalty for one's own people goes against what one knows and believes to be true, tension is the result. Every veteran of family conflict knows this kind of tension. It happens when parents see their children fighting. It happens when children see their parents fighting. It happens when Republicans or Democrats see their fellow party members fighting. In the antebellum years, tension was everywhere as the American family was split apart over the issue of slavery. State loyalties squared off with the voice of right reason with the result that in the South, "patriotism" succeeded in dethroning conscience. Being a son of Virginia was more important than being a son of the human race — black, white, red, or yellow.

The path to racial harmony today is a bit harder to define than it was in the 1860's. Then it was a matter of freeing the slaves. In our time, we see new kinds of prejudices awakening towards newly arrived immigrants. Now, more than ever, we are in need of a clarified sense of our American identity. We need something more powerful to unite people than the euphemistic, "Can't we all just get along?" Even the pious thought, "Most Americans are sons of former immigrants," does not have within it enough meaning to silence the voices which speak out for stricter enforcement of immigration laws. (Is there any other nation on earth that is so condemned for making rules about its borders?)

No one should enjoy conflict; but neither should conflict be resolved by pretense. The temptation always exists to declare disagreements unreal and imaginary, or that they can be resolved by the simple appeal for unity. Granted, a great many of society's conflicts would be resolved if warring factions just talked things over more, or sincerely listened to their opponent's perspective. But there are some problems that are not the result of misunderstandings, or ignorance of facts. Some opposing forces know exactly what the other is saying or doing. Such conflicts are a result of opposing fundamental convictions about the truth of human nature. They are incarnated manifestations of the real supernatural battle between good and evil, between the principalities and the powers.

The prospect of getting to the bottom of things and calling some things right and some things wrong is too hard for many contemporary Americans. Unprepared or unwilling to enter a philosophical discourse, we have accepted an "anything goes" philosophy. In the name of open mindedness, we have opted to avoid confrontation rather than insist on the pursuit of truth. Or, we "agree to disagree" and separate ourselves from one another to "preserve peace." Every divorce is a domestic excommunication on the part of former lovers. "You live in your world, and I'll live in mine." We fancy ourselves smart or progressive for "resolving" so many conflicts in this "peaceful" way without ever really appreciating that evil is winning tiny victories each time.

Fighting Spirit

On April 6, 1862, General Ulysses S. Grant was caught off guard by Confederate forces as he rested his troops near the country meeting house known as Shiloh Church, a little more than 20 miles from Corinth, Mississippi. In the two day battle that followed, the Union suffered 13,000 casualties; the Confederates, 10,700. Grant was unperturbed by the first day of fighting in which he lost practically all the ground he had held in the morning. "The enemy has done all he can do today. Tomorrow morning . . . we will soon finish him up." Grant's prediction proved true. The next day, the tide was turned and Shiloh became a decisive victory for the North, sending the Confederate control of the West on a permanent and inevitable downslide. But the staggering losses dismayed the press, Grant's superior officers, and many in Washington. A general call went out for Grant's removal. In response to such a suggestion from a prominent Republican, the President answered, "I can't spare this man; he fights."

Lincoln had good reason to value Grant's services. The greatest difficulty of the war effort had been the reluctance of Union generals to engage the enemy or follow up victories on the field with decisive pursuit and closure. Lincoln bewailed his officers' tactics: "They [the Northern officers] have got the idea into their heads that we are going to get out of this fix, somehow, by strategy! . . . That's the word — strategy! General McClellan thinks he is going to whip the rebels by strategy; and the army has got the same notion."[55]

At the head of the Union army was a dashing, expert administrator named George B. McClellan whose overcautious reckoning of rebel numbers kept him time and again from making the bold attacks that, unbeknown to him, the South expected and feared. For example, on the night of September

55. Donald, *Lincoln*, p. 389

*18, 1862, Lee withdrew his army from Sharpsburg,
site of the bloody battle of Antietam. McClellan let
him go and then failed to follow in the weeks after.
Lincoln, amazed and bewildered by McClellan's
inactivity, came himself to the scene to speak with
the general. The President left the unproductive
meeting and, walking with his friend O. M. Hatch,
pointed to the rows upon rows of army tents. He
asked Hatch what they were looking at. "Why, Mr.
Lincoln . . . this is the Army of the Potomac."
Lincoln replied, "No, Hatch, no. This is* General
McClellan's body-guard."[56]

General McClellan was only one of Lincoln's reluctant
generals. Halleck in the West also showed himself to be too slow
and too cautious. It took two years and several staff changes before
Lincoln got the men he needed in place — men with a fighting
spirit who wanted justice done and the war over quickly. The entire
scene shifted into gear as Sherman began his march to the sea and
Grant, refusing to take a licking, pressed Lee's Army of Northern
Virginia right up to Appomattox.

Lincoln had to sift through quite a batch of characters to find
the right formula for success. There were those who wanted to fight
— but for reasons of personal glory and gain. When they did not
see an effort adding anything to their personal fortune, they stood
still. There were those who disliked the very notion of the war and
wanted a return to the way things were before Fort Sumter. These
stalled every effort to get on the field hoping that discussion and
dialogue would bring an end to the matter without bloodshed. In
the end, it was only decisive military victory that ended the
rebellion, restored union, and left the country with a new policy of
emancipation.

In the abortion debate we see the same parties at play again.

---

56. Donald, *Lincoln*, p. 387

Some ride the political current with nothing in mind but their own promotion. Others do not want to be disturbed by the radical suggestions of the pro-life position. Lincoln's words about strategy could very well be a criticism of contemporary voices who respond to any sparks that fly from abortion related conflicts with the call for more "dialogue" in regard to the right to life. To paraphrase Lincoln's words again: "They think that the children will be saved by more dialogue, that's the word — dialogue!" Or, as Bishop Fabian Bruskewitz of Lincoln, Nebraska said in reference to the need for further dialogue regarding abortion (among other things), "It is impossible to imagine a dialogue between fire and the fire department."[57]

In matters such as slavery and abortion, the moderate position garners no praise. Respect is owed only to those who take a stand, be they right or wrong. The South may have erred about slavery, but history accords her soldiers the nod of approval for their zeal and courage. There were many officers in the Northern Army, but only the names of those who fought with determination and purpose ring in our memory: Grant, Sherman, Sheridan, Farragut. Thanks to the fighting spirit of these men, the issue of slavery was finally and thoroughly resolved. How long would slavery have lasted if the moderates had had their way? We have among us now some who have a real fighting spirit in defense of life. We have others who spend themselves tirelessly for what they believe to be a "woman's right." History will record the names of these antagonists either with praise or blame, but they certainly will not be forgotten. On the other hand, we have amongst us the "play it safe" moderates who would do well to think about the words of Jesus regarding the lukewarm, "I will spew you out of my mouth."

A False Pacifism

The parallel between the slavery issue and the abortion debate

---

57. *Pope Paul VI was a Prophet*, Catholic Dossier, Notre Dame University Press, vol. 3 no. 5 Sept. 1997, p. 13

can be seen in light of the fear that many moderate pro-lifers have regarding the intervention of the government in matters of sexual freedom. The fear of government intrusion into personal life was expressed by men such as William Seward, Clement Vallandigham and Justice Roger Brooke Taney. They could acknowledge that slavery was wrong — but to have the federal government passing laws making it a criminal activity . . . that was a violation of personal rights! Nowadays, we hold such a view in regards to slavery to be an expression of incredible ignorance. How could such blindness be possible, we wonder?

Yet, moderate pro-lifers have inherited the same myopia. They would agree that abortion is not a good, and they would say that they wish it wasn't going on; but this distaste is pitted against what they believe to be a threat to freedom, particularly freedom to live in a society where external factors do not inhibit one's sexual lifestyle. This is why the abortion question is seen to be "too complex," since it pits two important values against each other: life and freedom. By remaining conservative, that is to say, doing little to change the status quo regarding abortion laws, the value of freedom wins the day over life. The argument for this is rooted in such patriotic sentiments as "Give me liberty or give me death." Moderates are proud to take a certain militaristic attitude about the matter since good soldiers are willing to die in defense of freedom. The difficulty in this case is that they are operating with an incomplete idea of freedom since they have placed it above the right of innocent human beings to live. They have turned the whole argument upside down and made freedom the enemy of life.

Moderate pro-lifers are greatly frustrated by this conflict, but they view this battle as they view all of history's battles. "If we have learned anything in modern times," they argue, "it is that war is hell and that the ugly reality of war teaches us that there is no such thing as a good war." (As a student of the Civil War, I find this one of the dominant conclusions authors try to impress upon their readers.) Consequently, the moderate, believing himself to be a peaceable man, will not join forces with the radical pro-life side. That could provoke tension, controversy, and even open conflict. We want to avoid all of that.

Those who would take a moderate position on abortion should consider that a lie rests at the center of their convictions, a lie so seductively sweet that the bitter taste of evil is swallowed up by it. "We are true pacifists," says the lie. "We do not allow killing for any reason." Moderates flatter themselves that they are the real champions of life and that theirs is a genuine charity. Don't they, after all, prefer dialogue and persuasion to bitter conflict? What a sigh of self-approving contentment follows this assessment! If they could only see the body count that actually follows in its wake! But their eyes are turned away from the river of blood that has gathered around the nation's abortion mills.

The stance of the "social-liberal," proud to be both a pacifist and a supporter of abortion rights, is a gross contradiction. The true pacifist opposes all wars. The true pacifist denies the possibility of a "just war." Today's social-liberalism, however, maintains the just war theory as the backbone of its argument because it presumes the necessity of killing. "No one likes abortion," they say, "but those who have to have an abortion have good reasons." How can one claim an unqualified condemnation of killing while at the same time making an argument for abortion? As the saying goes, "You can't have your cake and eat it, too." Clearly, the moderate position ultimately places bloodshed over political negotiation. This is why both the radical pro-choice position as well as the moderate position unfairly claim a pacifist mentality while a war rages around them and the body count escalates.

In Their Own Words

The Civil War was a time of speeches, letters, and diaries. Each side had its orators and poets. The profundity of some of this literature echoes down through the ages. Oddly enough, however, most of the most emotionally charged quotes from the war are absent in Civil War books. This is, of course, another example of the desire to wear value-free spectacles when we look at that nation-defining event and to protect citizens of the North or South from responding emotionally to history. But, we need to feel some passion about the Civil War in order to really appreciate it. Too often I have found the feeling of Civil War buffs for their subject comes from an interest in uniforms, guns, and battlefields rather than the fundamental issues at stake.

I would like to present you with some of the "missing links" of Civil War rhetoric — not with the purpose of belittling the South, or the North, for that matter, but to illustrate the profoundly different views of human nature and the meaning of life, the different creeds, if you will, that were held so strongly by Americans at that time. For many, the following quotes are going to be hard to read. It may be thought that no good can come from repeating them. But, to paraphrase St. Jerome's comment on the scriptures, "To be ignorant of the Civil War is to be ignorant of America."

So close your eyes and make a fist if you must, but listen to some of the passion that lay behind the battles whose names have passed into our heritage.

Southerners hardly ever used the words "slavery" or "slave." They spoke of "our own institutions" and "the nigger." In those two words is summed up the Southern cause: to maintain control of an economic system based on the racial supremacy of the white man. Clever politicians learned to pick up Southern vocabulary. Stephen Douglas, for example, defended the South's "right to choose their own social institutions."[58]

Listen to these words, written by a North Carolina officer as he stopped in Gettysburg for a meal: "They live in real Yankee style — wives and daughters and a help do all the work. It makes me more than ever devoted to our own Southern institutions."

---

58. James M. McPherson, *What They Fought For, 1861-1865* (Baton Rouge and London: Louisiana State University Press, 1994), p. 52

Or take this Confederate private's remark, less than a year before Lee surrendered at Appomattox: "We are sure of victory because we are fighting for our property and homes; they [the North] for the flimsy and abstract idea that a Negro is equal to an Anglo American."[59]

Southerners spoke often of defending their property. It's easy for us to forget that the property in question was not their lands or their homes, but men, women, and children. Jefferson Davis, supposedly "personally opposed" to slavery, justified secession as an act of self-defense against Black Republicans whose efforts would make "property in slaves so insecure as to be comparatively worthless . . . thereby annihilating in effect property worth thousands of millions of dollars."[60] The boy-colonel, 21 year old Col. Henry Burgwyn, wrote to his father, "I would buy boys and girls from 15 to 20 years old and take care to have a majority of girls. The increase in number of your Negroes by this means would repay the difference in the amount of available labor. I would not be surprised to see Negroes in six months after peace, worth from $2,000 to $3,000."[61] Col. Burgwyn never realized these profits. He was killed at Gettysburg.

Even non-slaveholding Southerners had to side with those who did own slaves. These poorer Southerners: " . . . emphasized a form of property they did own, one that was central to the liberty for which they fought. That property was their white skins, which put them on a plane of civil equality with slave holders and far above those who did not possess that property."[62]

A South Carolina son wrote to his family: "I despise the cost of freeing the black devils. No less than 300,000 of our own free white citizens have already been sacrificed to free the small mite

---

59. McPherson, *What They Fought For, 1861-1865*, p. 56
60. McPherson, *What They Fought For, 1861-1865*, p. 47
61. McPherson, *What They Fought For, 1861-1865*, p. 49
62. McPherson, *What They Fought For, 1861-1865*, p. 52

that have got their freedom . . . I consider the life and happiness of my family of more value than any nigger."[63]

A note from a Union soldier of the 6th Kentucky shows just how much conversion was needed in the hearts of the men in blue. He wished that "old Abe Lincoln . . . had to sleep with a Negro every night as long as he lives and kiss one's ass twice a day."[64]

We might be able to dismiss such backward thinking if these were words of some far away ancient culture, but these are Americans, not so long ago, so we should be a little uneasy about them. Nor should we assume that Union soldiers were innocent of such prejudice. Consider some of these quotes from the army of the blue.

These quotes are important to absorb because they prove that leaders were desperately needed within the ranks to keep at front and center the real issue that had provoked the war. Such leaders were available. Many letters from Union men reveal that their authors were very conscious of the true nature of the war and their role in it. In words that seem to capture the essence of everything good about America, these letters reveal a profound solidarity and compassion for the slaves and a willingness to do all that was necessary to make freedom the law of the land.

We can derive a great lesson of leadership from these men. While the President in the Capital was holding out against racism at the highest political level, on the battlefield the common solider who held abolitionist views faced the same tensions. There were leaders in the trenches of Gettysburg as there were leaders in the halls of Congress. However, these men did not lead in the contemporary sense of giving political speeches; rather, they fought bravely for a cause that was not universally appreciated and by the strength and sincerity of their witness they pulled others

---

63. McPherson, *What They Fought For, 1861-1865*, p. 63
64. McPherson, *What They Fought For, 1861-1865*, p. 67

along with them. Who can say how many conversions took place because of conversations during long, boring marches or around evening campfires?

I can't help but quote again from James McPherson's extensive research of soldiers' letters. Can you imagine the effect a soldier like this had on his fellow racist soldiers? "I have no heart in this war if the slaves cannot go free . . . Our cause is nobler even than the Revolution, for they fought for their own freedom, while we fight for that of another race . . . If the doom of slavery is not sealed by the war I shall curse the day I entered the Army or lifted a finger in the preservation of the Union."[65]

All Civil War commentators recognize most Northern soldiers were at first ambivalent to the slavery issue. Eventually, though, many came to have a change of heart. For example, an antebellum Douglas Democrat wrote his wife in 1863 that his regiment had confiscated horses and liberated hundreds of slaves in middle Tennessee. "Now what do you think of your husband degenerating from a conservative young Democrat to a horse stealer and a 'nigger thief'?" He asked her playfully. Then in a later letter he tells her, "So long as my flag is confronted by the hostile guns of slavery . . . I am as confirmed an abolitionist as ever was pelted with stale eggs."[66]

Though fundamental to the outcome of the war, the conversion of many a Northerner to the cause of emancipation rarely receives attention. A remarkable exception to this is the movie *Glory* — a must see for all Americans. As the casualty list grew longer, it became evident to both sides that the large number of available African-American males could be a deciding factor. Clearly, the South had difficulty justifying the use of Negro soldiers in the defense of a cause that meant their continued enslavement. For the North, however, the appearance of black regiments marked the

---

65. McPherson, *What They Fought For, 1861-1865*, p. 56
66. McPherson, *What They Fought For, 1861-1865*, p. 67

beginning of a change in the social perception of the African-American as a citizen. Civil War specialist Bruce Catton comments on the formation of black regiments:

> *To this the soldiers made a good deal of objection — at first. Then they began to change their minds. They did not like the Negroes, for race prejudice of a malignity rarely seen today was very prevalent in the North and they did not want to associate with them on anything remotely like terms of equality . . . [But through the fighting] they realized that the colored soldier could stop a Rebel bullet just as well as a white soldier could, and when he did so, some white soldier who would otherwise have died would go on living . . . And so by the middle of 1863 the North was raising Negro regiments, and the white soldiers who had been so bitter about the idea adjusted themselves rapidly.*"[67]

From what we have just seen, the men who fought in the Civil War were not unconscious of their motivations or the issues at stake. Since they have expressed themselves so clearly, we should not hesitate to listen to them with attention and discernment. It would discredit them to pretend that they were clumsy pawns of their "higher ups." It dishonors them to avoid the content of their convictions. It honors them to say "this is what they believed," and it gives credit to us to follow up with the judgement, "this was right" or "this was wrong." We must not be afraid that such a judgement means we do not love our Confederate ancestors or that we have no respect for their courage and dedication. At the same time, we must not give ourselves over to a sentimentality that would love to make heroes of everyone. Like the men who wrote the letters above, we must choose sides.

---

67. Bruce Catton, *The Civil War* (New York, NY: American Heritage Press, 1971), p. 190

The Sweetheart Principle

Another insight we can glean from Civil War letters and diaries is the misunderstanding that surrounded the emancipation cause. For example, after talking with a captured Confederate soldier, a Wisconsin private wrote about how baffled he was when the soldier answered his question "Why you Rebs fighten'?" Said the Confederate, "You Yanks want us to marry our daughters to the niggers."[68]

The parallel between this quote and today's abortion debate may be a bit difficult to see, but it is certainly present. I mean to say that at times certain pro-choicers will look at pro-lifers and say something very reminiscent. It's eerie, but believe me, it's true. They will say things like: "You pro-lifers want to take all the fun out of life. You don't want people to enjoy sex but have everyone live as monks."

This is a classic example of reading too much into your opponent's position. A wise Northern soldier might have replied to his misinformed prisoner, "Freeing the slaves does not mean your sisters have to marry one." The one event does not lead necessarily to the other. Pro-lifers need to let pro-choicers know that they have no intention of making everyone live like monks or taking the fun out of sex. To be pro-life does not represent a return to the sexual mores of Victorian times — surely one of the hidden fears of every pro-choicer. On the contrary, pro-life couples are hardly a paradigm for celibacy, as the size of most pro-life families will prove. But then, the pro-life mindset maintains the union between sex and life. When pro-choicers complain about taking the fun out of sex, what they really mean is that sex is no fun when it may result in a new human life. To push the matter even further, abortion is a symbol of sexual freedom in general. The proof of this is its defense by those who are no longer or will never be in a position to have an

68. McPherson, *What They Fought For, 1861-1865*, p. 53

abortion: homosexuals, for instance, or women past childbearing years. Their enthusiasm for legalized abortion flows from their fear that if *Roe v. Wade* were reversed, the government would then enact other legislation to restrict one's sexual freedom even further.

The misunderstanding that surrounded the emancipation question was the result of what I like to call "The Sweetheart Principle." That is, all great conflicts sooner or later get down to some aspect of a man's sweetheart. Simply stated, this principle is based on the fact that a man's philosophy of a happy life contains the simple but profound formula: a man wants to do nice things with his nice girl with nice stuff. As long as he feels he is able to follow this basic law of nature he is satisfied. But, upset this condition in some way, and someone's gonna get hurt.

Recall General Pickett's last minute pep talk at Gettysburg before his men in gray began their ill-fated charge: "For your wives, for your daughters, for your sweethearts, for Virginia!" Obviously, there would not be much reason for fighting for Virginia if it were not for the fact that Virginia is a nice place where they get nice things for their women. More than anything else, they did not want their sweethearts to have to work like slaves. And who could blame them? What gentleman worth his salt would? They, like most people of the world, believed that they worked hard to get where they were. No one was going to force them to give all those nice things up.

This Arkansas captain captures the spirit of the sweetheart principle quite well: "If the Yanks win, our sisters, wives, and mothers are to be given up to the embraces of their present dusky male servitors."[69] Another, not grasping the contradiction of his words, wrote: "The deep still quiet peace of the grave is more desirable than vassalage or slavery." We must "die as free men or live as slaves," better far "to die rather than be slaves."[70]

---

69. McPherson, *What They Fought For, 1861-1865*, p. 53
70. McPherson, *What They Fought For, 1861-1865*, p. 50

The Southerners reasoned they were fighting for the same liberty for which their ancestors died in the 1770's. In a sense they were. But even back in the Revolutionary War days, Samuel Johnson pointed out an important philosophical contradiction. In 1775 he wrote, "How is it that we hear the loudest yelps to liberty among the drivers of Negroes?" It's frightening, but the mindset of the antebellum South seems to have survived the war and the passage of time. With the alteration of but a few words, we could use Johnson's question for the pro-choice crowd today: "How is that we hear the loudest yelps to liberty among the killers of babies?"

The Confederate as Hero

Americans are justified in finding much to admire in the Confederate soldier. For one thing, every Confederate knew he was fighting for something beyond himself. He would have summed up his convictions by calling himself a son of Virginia, or Georgia, or South Carolina. He felt that everything he held dear in this world was within his own state lines — his land, his family, his culture — and he was willing to pay the highest price for the protection of these goods.

For us, the term "state" does not have the same weight it did for Americans of the mid-19th century. At that time, the echo of the colonial period was still strong. The united effort of the colonies — the first states, if you will — brought about independence from Great Britain. The term chosen to designate this new country — "The United States" — captured the sense of liberty and autonomy belonging to each of the states. In the years following the Revolution, however, more and more power went into the hands of the federal government. Slavery became an issue that tested not only the moral fiber of the country but the shape and means of its governance. The Confederacy represented a last attempt to preserve the unqualified control of each state over affairs within its borders.

Those who chose to remain with the Confederacy believed themselves to be supremely patriotic. Robert E. Lee is a case in point. On April 18, 1861, Lee was summoned to Washington and offered command of a new army being formed to force the seceded states back into the Union. Lee opposed slavery and secession, but he also opposed a war that would subject the states to the will of the federal government. Lee resigned from the United States Army in which he had served for thirty-six years. His reason: he could not abandon his country — that is, his native state of Virginia.

Such devotion to the land in which one is born and bred is understandable. On the other hand, we cannot settle the issue at this level alone. We must not forget that Lee erred — and gravely. It would be simple to say that he chose the state of Virginia and leave it at that. What is difficult is to accept the fact that in choosing Virginia he abandoned convictions that should have been deeper than his love for his state. He abandoned the fundamental right of every human being to self-determination. His heroism did not extend as far as standing up against his culture for human rights. He was a Virginian hero, but he was not and can never be an international hero, a hero whose virtues can be seen across cultures and down the ages.

There are many present-day Americans who want to praise and cheer the Confederacy while simultaneously ignoring the South's radical racist philosophy. The contemporary moral relativism of American culture, clumsily translated as "tolerance," seems to demand that we refrain from any praise or blame. We have a difficult time calling the Northerners the good guys and the Southerners the bad guys. But how can we claim to be against racism if we do not qualify our praise of Robert E. Lee and company in one way or another? Admire their courage, yes. Praise their willingness to sacrifice their lives for a cause greater than themselves, yes. But ignore the fundamental error of their choice by making all things relative — thus losing the great advancement to society that Lincoln and the Union troops won for our nation — hardly.

Those who want to praise the South solely for standing up for what they believe, or for fighting for the right of self-governance, fail to appreciate that sincerity is not enough of a reason to approve of someone's actions when those actions do grave harm. A doctor may be very sincere when he mistakenly gives a patient the wrong medicine, but his sincerity will not save him from judgement if the patient dies. There are many sincere abortion advocates out there — but that doesn't change the fact that they are responsible for millions of lost lives.

The hesitancy to offer accurate praise and blame regarding Civil War figures only proves that we are willing to compromise the value content of human action in favor of sentiment. Of course, a beautiful sentiment can be hidden in the hesitancy to raise the hand of the North high in victory: the kindness of a brother, not wanting to gloat in a victory over his own brother. At the same time, however, for educational purposes, it is important to separate the sheep from the goats during the time of the Civil War and learn what was ultimately praiseworthy and blameworthy. Otherwise, we lose the vital energy that keeps this nation from abandoning her founding principles.

Society today says we must not study our history lessons with 20th century prejudices. We have been primed to be non-judgmental about the Civil War, to pick out no villains and no heroes, to sweep under the carpet any suggestion of moral error. This is an unfortunate consequence. Those who would promote non-judgmental thinking about the Civil War may not realize that a consequence of not making negative judgements is the inability to make positive judgements as well. To say Abraham Lincoln or Frederick Douglas or Joshua Chamberlain were heroes is to render a judgement. Society always looks for heroes — but we cannot have any if there are no villains. Heroes and villains become indistinguishable in a non-judgmental history. A dearth of them is another casualty of such moral relativism.

Perhaps our focus on the Civil War has been dulled by the

success of civil rights since that time. There are very few true racists in the spotlight anymore. When they exist, they are quickly turned into caricature. Enough credit is not given to the Southerners of today for so powerfully transforming their culture. True enough, post-war Southern states had a difficult time stamping out racism — but successes in this effort can certainly be acknowledged. Racial prejudice, where it still exists, knows no geographic boundaries. One can see that racial prejudice is as much an issue in the North as in the South these days.

Northern heroes can also be lost in the non-judgmental light of current historicism. Some would say that our Northern heroes were great simply because they fought to save the Union. But to make this claim is to fall into the trap of praising these men simply for maintaining the size of the nation as if somehow size is the only benchmark of greatness. This is a bit like a man who praises a shoe simply because it is a big shoe. Certainly, the bigness of a shoe is praiseworthy if it is for a big foot, but it becomes quite a problem if one has a small foot. Shoe size is relative. The greatness of a nation is not determined by size, either. A nation's constitution and the way it promotes the dignity of the human person are the true determinations of greatness.

We Americans today are citizens of a big and powerful country. Why do we take pride in its greatness, its bigness and power? Are we infatuated with bigness and power for their own sake? People who were willing to kill other human beings to accumulate property are usually considered tyrants and megalomaniacs. Consider the attempts of Napoleon or Hitler. Aggrandizement alone is not enough. But if the Civil War meant more territory for a greater justice, then we have something about which we can justifiably feel proud.

What is needed today is another way of expressing love for the Confederacy while simultaneously denouncing racism. I believe this to be a very important point and not just an academic question for historians to debate. The way one settles this philosophical inconsistency greatly effects the way one deals with conflicts and divisions of today. It is just as important for Northerners as it is for Southerners of today to settle this dysfunctional intellectualism, this philosophical torture, if we truly desire progress.

Another Kind of Spirit

Fighting spirit is not enough to insure the triumph of a just cause. Where justice and peace meet, kindness and truth also embrace. We may have to face the enemy with zeal on the field, but we must not forget that it is his cause we despise and not his person. The Christian adage "Love the sinner — hate the sin" still holds today.

But the Christian love of which I speak is itself a challenge for a morally relativistic culture because it has this important characteristic: it is lived within a truth about human nature that can be known. Few people today are willing to acknowledge such a notion. It seems too dogmatic — to threatening to personal liberty. Still, there is no way around it. Love without truth is impossible. That is why a culture that denies objective truth makes love of neighbor more difficult. In a sense, one is forced into a lie that ultimately harms the neighbor. Pro-abortion advocates will say that they love women and all their efforts are for their good, but the love to which they appeal is a fiction. Love and lies are mutually exclusive. You cannot say, "I love you" to someone while you are simultaneously sticking a knife in their back. Abortion is such a crime against women as well as their unborn children that one has to wonder what this word "love" has really come to mean in our time.

This is how the popular argument goes: divisions are made worse when fighting parties hold to "their own" view, to their own sense of the so-called objective truth. One side must let go of its point of view for peace to be restored. This letting go is usually to be done by the party insisting on a moral standard. Somehow a moral standard is more threatening to society than the absence of a moral standard. Those who would insist on a right and wrong must learn the higher road of "tolerance" — the greatest virtue and the most misunderstood and misapplied virtue of our time.

True enough, tolerance is an extremely important virtue when it comes to maintaining peace and loving your enemy. However, when tolerance is preached on the pretense that truth is relative, it renders useless any kind of meaningful dialogue. No advance can be made towards unity. Such a tactic is popular in the hands of those who would like to maintain control of a situation when they are clearly on the side of injustice. The Confederacy did as much during the second half of the Civil War when their military victories became fewer and fewer. In the North they were supported by the "Peace Democrats" who attacked Lincoln as a tyrant and an instigator of violence. They proposed leaving the South in peace — with their slaves, that is.

Bruce Catton speaks more profoundly than I think he realizes when he says, "By the middle of the nineteenth century slavery was too fragile for that. It could exist only by the tolerance of people who did not like it, and war destroyed that tolerance."[71] He makes the crucial almost heart-stopping connection between "tolerance" and the perpetuation of an evil. The tolerance that is proposed to us is a false friend when it suggests the abandonment of objective truth and the acceptance that truth is relative. A hidden agenda of despair lies behind this pseudo-tolerance. In so many words it tells us, "The search for truth is impossible — it can't be found. You will only suffer more divisions and arguments if you try." There is no hope of human beings finding unity in an agreement of common moral principles. But even if one particular truth in this area or that area of human life is too hard for some to swallow, let us at least agree that Americans should be on a quest for the truth. For when we as a nation consider even the quest for truth an attack on society we plant the seeds of our own destruction.

---

71. Catton, *The Civil War*, p. 188

This is, of course, a dangerous game. The rhetoric of tolerance becomes a tool of oppression in the hands of the powerful. If truth is relative, what is to check human greed? Think about it. What better argument could you have to preserve the status quo for slavery or abortion than that all opinions are just that, opinions, with no substance or power to command human affairs. Slaves and their abolitionist friends held the opinion that the African-American is a person. They believed this was an objective, self-evident truth. It was to the interest of the slave owners, on the other hand, to believe that "everything's relative." Though we may never stumble on this argument in the writings of the time, relativism was certainly the fuel that kept the Confederate campfires burning.

True tolerance is far from moral relativism. Working within the context of objective truth, it allows for the time and dialogue necessary for conversion to take place. It respects the dignity of the erring party by allowing them to come to the truth on their own and freely accept the right path. Tolerance does not imply the subjection of one person or group of people to another. It stands for the common ground where all may find sanctuary and brotherhood. In this light, we can look with affection on our Confederate brothers and sisters. They labored under a profound ignorance — perhaps culpable, but probably more often than not beyond their ability to overcome. This same ignorance plays a part in our moral evaluation of Northern soldiers who did not fight to free the slaves, but under compulsion or self-interest, or for the lesser glory of preserving a big nation.

What is the spirit of the true tolerance that leads to conversion and unity? How do we love someone even when we know them to be incredibly wrong, even when they are trying to do us great harm? There is only one way. It is the way of Jesus. Even as He was being crucified, he prayed, "Father, forgive them, for they know not what they do." In this context, too, pro-lifers can find room in their hearts to love their ideological enemies. Although it is impossible for some of us to imagine, there are some who do not see the obvious contradiction between fighting for "choice" and the complete denial of granting the unborn a right to choose anything at all. There are abortionists and abortion clinic personnel who, for one reason or another, are blind to the true nature of their work. We know conversions are possible. Who is not moved by the testimony of Dr. Bernard Nathanson — who claimed to have assisted at tens of thousands of abortions either directly or indirectly, or Norma McCorvey — the original Jane Roe of *Roe v. Wade*? How many prayers have been said for these individuals? How many sacrifices made? Only Heaven knows. But one thing is for certain: conversions do not happen by accident. Somewhere, sometime, a fighting spirit went out to face the enemy, armed with truth and the power of love.

The Heart of the Matter

The casualty lists of war force the question upon us: what is the value of a single human life? In a civil war, where brother slays brother, this query is heightened by the realization that even the ties of family, friendship and land are not enough to insure reverence for human life. Overwhelmed by the voices of self-interest and pride, that which should be strongest in us becomes the faintest whisper in our conscience. We forget who and what we are; hence, war becomes the tragic re-awakening of our memory. It re-sensitizes mankind by carving out images too strong for reason to withstand. At least for a moment, we feel once again the fragility of life and are drawn back into its service.

One of the most touching aspects of the Civil War story is the record of this personal odyssey of spiritual awakening left to us by men and women on both sides of the conflict. Some of these writings come from the pen of the gifted and cultured, some from the simple and unschooled. Yet, something rings in them and calls to us from across the years. For the first time, the unbounded optimism of an infant nation was temporarily suspended as Americans faced together the hard truths of the human condition, realizing in a kind of dazed fashion at times, that these perennial realities would not be overcome by unbounded territories, material prosperity and a new form of governance. Something more was going to be required if the nation would survive and realize the promise of her founding. Something would have to counter that fateful day in 1857 when a human being stood before the highest court of the land and seven of the seated justices saw only a piece of property. Where one would have expected an increase in enlightenment and justice, the Supreme Court showed itself to have regressed further back than the Magna Carter.

I am referring, of course, to the Supreme Court decision in *Dred Scott v. Sandford*. Most people are aware that the *Dred Scott* decision had something to do with keeping slavery legal in the United States, but most do not know the exact origins of the case which did not begin as an attempt to resolve the slavery issue. The original case consisted of Dred Scott's suit against his owner, John F. A. Sanford, on three counts of assault — one against Dred Scott himself, one against his wife, and one against his children. Dred Scott's case rested on the contention that because of the Missouri Compromise Dred Scott had become a free man when he entered the state of Illinois (a free state) with his master in 1834. This period had also been followed by some time in the free territory of Wisconsin. In 1846, back in Missouri, Dred Scott enlisted the aid of anti-slavery lawyers who sued for his freedom on the grounds that his residence in a free state and a free territory had made him a free man. The Missouri Supreme Court overturned an initially favorable ruling by a lower court. From there, the long trail started towards the United States Supreme Court.

The final ruling that came down from the Supreme Court of the United States on March 6, 1857 far exceeded the case itself. The term "watershed" is used to describe such decisions since they represent a radical turning point for judicial review. Not only was Dred Scott's entire case swept aside on the basis of the belief that he was still a slave, but the court went on to rule that no African-American could claim citizenship in the United States. The decision was written by Chief Justice Roger Brooke Taney:

> *The question is simply this: Can a negro, whose ancestors were imported into this country and sold as slaves, become a member of the political community formed and brought into existence by the constitution of these United States and as such become entitled to all the rights, and privileges, immunities, guaranteed by that instrument to the citizen? ... The words "people of the United States" and "citizens" are synonymous terms, and mean the same thing. They both describe a political body who, according to our republican institutions, form the sovereignty, and who hold the power and conduct the government through their representatives. They are what we familiarly call the "sovereign people,*

and every citizen is one of this people, and a constituent member of this sovereignty. The question before us is, whether the class of persons described in the plea abatement compose a portion of this people, and are constituent members of this sovereignty? We think they are not, and that they are not included, and were not intended to be included, under the word "citizens" in the constitution, and can therefore claim none of the rights and privileges which that instrument provides for and secures to citizens of the United States. On the contrary, they were at that time considered as a subordinate and inferior class of beings, who had been subjugated by the dominant race, and, whether emancipated or not, yet remained subject to their authority, and had no rights or privileges . . .

Furthermore, since property rights were assured under the Fifth Amendment of the Constitution, the Court ruled that no intervention of Congress or a territorial legislature could affect slavery in the states — a clear victory for the slaveholding South:

Upon these considerations it is the opinion of the court that the act of Congress which prohibited a citizen from holding and owning property of this kind [African-Americans] in the territory of the United States north of the line therein mentioned is not warranted by the Constitution and is therefore void; and that neither Dred Scott himself, nor any of his family, were made free by being carried into this territory; even if they had been carried there by the owner with the intention of becoming a permanent resident.

One hundred and fifty years later we find it easy to castigate Chief Justice Taney and his court. We have no problem calling their decision shameful, their motivations corrupt, their understanding clouded by prejudice, ambition, and greed. So easy to do. Yet, we live under the shadow of a court ruling more perverse than that passed down to Dred Scott.

In 1973 the Supreme Court abandoned the nation's offspring, handing them over to butchers and profiteers. Seven of the nine justices who heard *Roe v. Wade* silenced their own humanity and betrayed their judicial responsibility. Who can look at a picture of the Burger court, of these solemn figures in their black robes, and keep from shuddering? Black becomes them. If the blood of one brother cries to God from the ground, what of the blood of forty million?

But notice how the numbers, the unimaginable numbers, themselves desensitize us to the horror of abortion. Joseph Stalin once said, "One death is a tragedy; a million deaths is a statistic." Truly, we are numbed by the immensity of it all. What will it take for us to put on mourning? Perhaps the daily newspapers should list the names of every child killed by abortion just as they listed the names of every soldier killed in the battles of the Civil War. Maybe that way we could blow the cover off abortion as an impersonal event and wake people up to the fact that real human beings are dying.

The Death of Innocence

"[A]nother ball came and struck the foreleg of a beautiful bay horse belonging to an officer on General Hooker's staff. It smashed the entire leg from the breast to the hoof. The poor horse jerked back, broke the halter-strap, fell on his back, then recovered himself, arose and hobbled away on three legs, dangling the hoof of the fourth leg, which was held suspended by a strip of skin. This strip of skin, about two inches wide, and the hoof were all that remained of the fore-leg. Blood flowed profusely and stained the ground wherever he passed. He was soon shot and put out of pain. I hardly remember a sight that touched my heart so keenly during the entire battle. The innocent animal had no part in the fight, but he was a silent victim."[72]

This passage comes from the Civil War memoirs of Father William Corby, chaplain for the Irish Brigade of the Union Army and eyewitness to the battle of Chancellorsville. In this major battle of the war, 190,000 men were involved; 29,000 lost their lives. The fallen included the heroic Southern general T.J. "Stonewall" Jackson — shot by mistake by his own men. Throughout the winter, the two opposing armies had faced each other from across the Rapahanuc River. When the time to move arrived, commanding Union General Joseph Hooker hoped to encircle and destroy the Confederate Army of Northern Virginia under Robert E. Lee. Due to Lee's swift and ingenious action, Chancellorsville became another Union opportunity lost.

Father Corby was present for it all. After accompanying his brigade through several bold attacks and the loss of many men, he went with his surgeons to the field hospital that also served as General Hooker's headquarters. He was tending to the wounded there when the Confederates located the command area and began a furious bombardment. Father Corby watched the carnage unfold around him. As General Hooker was following the progress of the battle from the porch of the house, a shell obliterated the pillar upon which he was leaning. He suffered a terrible concussion in the blast. Another shell sent the bricks of the chimney flying, and another killed a soldier trying to quench his thirst at the well. As the bombs continued to fall, Father Corby and the others found themselves in the dilemma of seeking their own safety or staying with the wounded. It was then that the priest beheld the wounding of the beautiful bay horse.

---

72. William Corby, C.S.C., *Memoirs of Chaplain Life*, ed. Lawrence Frederick Kohl (New York, NY: Fordham University Press, 1992), p. 160

Father Corby was no wimp. He was a hero in every sense of the term who did honor to his country, his church, and his profession during his service in the Union Army. He was present at some of the most important and pivotal actions of the Civil War and his benediction of the Catholic troops just before their engagement at Gettysburg is commemorated there with a statue, the same statue which stands at Notre Dame University where he served as president after the war. Yet, Father Corby's wartime experiences and manly heart did not mean the death of his humanity. He wrote without apology and with great sensitivity about the suffering of an animal, who "had no part in the fight, but was a silent victim."

Father Corby was no modern animal rights activist who often seem to value animal life more than human life. He did not suffer from that odd and profoundly disturbing ideology of many who are so protective of baby seals and whales but completely indifferent to the systematic extermination of human beings; those who are so moved by accounts of cruel and unnecessary animal slaughter or experimentation, but insensitive to the torments of a baby ripped apart in the womb, or kept alive for fetal experimentation. Father Corby was not one of these. He simply showed himself to possess a heart of flesh, not stone. He responded to the beauty and innocence of the bay horse, and felt the indignation that follows the unjust slaughter of such a victim.

Catholic teaching has always indicated that guilt and innocence are attributes belonging to persons, and that creation suffers because of the evil brought about by human action. According to scripture, the first of all such actions was the original sin of Adam and Eve in which the first parents chose to disobey God. Since then, history has logged the long account of man's selfishness played out continually in his abuse of nature for his own interests. Even so, mankind feels itself drawn to the innocence of nature, as our own American poets of the transcendental period so beautifully illustrate. Something of our former paradisiacal condition calls to us from nature. Animals seem to possess an innocence that we know we lack or have wounded by our choices.

Another powerful story from Father Corby's memoirs is that of the final moments of a 19-year-old soldier condemned to death for desertion. One of the chaplain's men came to tell him of the execution which was but a few hours away. Father Corby hurriedly went to the prisoner and found that he was under the care of a Methodist minister who had encouraged the boy's faith, but no more. Father Corby talked for awhile with the young man and discovered that he was of German descent, that his parents were probably Methodists, but that he himself had never been baptized. After a brief consultation with the minister, Father Corby baptized the prisoner, who was terribly afraid to die, and consoled him with the meaning of Christ's redemption and the promise of eternal life:

> *"Now you are a Christian; offer your life to God in union with the sufferings of Christ on the cross." For the first time I noticed a genuine softening in his disposition, as the light of faith, secured to him by the sacrament, seemed to show in his countenance. He had only a few moments to live, and when the squad of armed men came to escort him to death, he went out as coolly as if he were going to dinner . . . Eleven bullets struck the young man; still he was not dead. The provost-marshal was obliged to use his own revolver, to put him out of pain. Scenes like this jarred my nerves much more than a battle. And now, when more than a quarter of a century has passed since this took place, it causes a shuddering sensation to think of it; still more to write all the circumstances of such a dreadful spectacle.* [73]

Both the accounts above should move us deeply. That of the young solider more so. Why? We know him. He is a person to us.

---

73. Corby, *Memoirs of Chaplain Life*, pp. 122-127

We know his age, his nationality, and something about his religious background. We know he had his doubts about the war, and that he was a frail human being like ourselves who made a fatal mistake. He paid for it with his life. His story is made even more poignant by the fact that his own men killed him. He stood defenseless before eight or ten thousand who were lined up to watch him shot down by a squad of twelve. He may have been guilty of deserting to the enemy, but he was not in the act of hurting anyone at the moment of his death. It seems too cold-blooded — a punishment not in proportion to the crime. Such stories are common enough in war, yet twenty-five years later Father Corby still suffered a nervous trembling because of this one.

I have selected these two passages from Father Corby's memoirs to illustrate a kind of sensitivity to life that is necessary for clear thinking on issues such as abortion. We need to feel the "wrongness" of these situations, just as Father Corby did. Let us examine ourselves. Does the image of abortion raise any kind of response in us?

Instinctively, we should sense that to have an abortion or to promote legalized abortion requires a certain separation of heart and head. For a pregnant woman in crisis, alone with her fear and faced with apparently insurmountable difficulties, this is usually what happens. Abortion presents itself as the answer; later, the awful truth comes to her, sometimes with severe consequences. We have already spoken of Post-Abortion Stress Syndrome. But on the political level such an emotional crisis does not exist. Some kind of justification has to be found to separate heart and head and smother the voice of natural human feeling. The first attempt at such a rationale was the argument that a fetus is not a person — merely a conglomeration of cells and tissues. One could say that in the late 1960's there may have been enough doubt about the personhood of a fetus to overturn existing laws protecting the unborn and eventually carry the Supreme Court decision in *Roe v. Wade* of 1973. Thanks to advances in pre-natal science, such a position is now absurd.

Consider what we know now of life in the womb:

The child, from the very beginning, is its own separate being — not "part of" the mother. At the moment of fertilization, cellular development begins and heads in a specific direction; the sex of the child, for example, is already determined. At seventeen days the embryo has its own blood cells, and by eighteen days one can detect the pulsation of muscles that within a week will become the child's heart. The eyes begin to develop by day nineteen and the foundation of the entire nervous system is in place by the next day. Clearly, abortion is not the simple scraping away of lifeless, insensate matter. The tiny human being can feel the secure warmth of the womb as well as the pitiless lacerations of abortion.

In less than eight weeks the child grows 10,000 times itself to 6-7 mm (1/4 inch) long. This phenomenal activity is not a push from the outside but a result of a dynamic within the unborn child itself. By his one month anniversary of conception, the child's blood is flowing, his muscles are showing and his arms, legs, ears and nose have begun to grow. By day thirty-five the pituitary gland in the brain is forming. The skeleton is complete by the forty-second day and reflexes are present as the brain begins to coordination muscle and organ movement. Brain waves can be recorded by the forty-third day.

In less than two months the child appears to be complete in his physical form: fingers and toes, ears and lips. He even shows family traits in his features and is sensitive to touch. By day fifty-six the child's sitting height measures about three centimeters (1 1/8 inch) and he is about 1/30 ounce in weight. All his parts are in place and his organs functioning. From here on end he will merely continue to grow in size and strength.

Let us remember that we are speaking of the unborn child within the first trimester — the very period in which *Roe v. Wade* allowed abortion on demand. Life in the womb is not merely potential. A human being is present and a daily drama of activity, experiences, and learning is taking place. By the tenth week the child can squint and swallow, retract his tongue, grasp objects in his palm, and suck his thumb. By the eleventh week he is smiling. He can make a fist. He even has fingernails. At four months the mother is starting to feel her child's movements as he swims around in his amniotic sac, kicking her from time to time, and doing somersaults. He will react to loud noises or high frequencies — even those too high for adults to hear. By the eighteenth week he has vocal cords, and if he but had some air we would hear him cry. By twenty weeks, he weighs a solid pound and has about twelve inches in height. Hair begins to appear on his head.

Amazing, is it not? One has to ask how *Roe v. Wade* has been able to survive such information. If we show a man that two plus two equals four and he continues to insist that it equals five, we would have to conclude he is either mentally unable to comprehend or willfully resisting what he knows to be the truth. Either way, he is a dangerous man to have around.

The point is that today, with the information we now have about human life in the womb, we cannot plead ignorance. Indeed, we find ourselves in the strange situation of possessing too much knowledge. Clearly, our laws are not up to date. But do they even want to be? I would argue that the advances of pre-natal science now allow us to drop the charade of pretending abortion is only a matter of personal choice. It has never really been about choice, and the personhood of the fetus has never really been the issue.

Legalized abortion is and always has been about the rights of one group of human beings over another.

I cannot help but be amazed at the similarity in the arguments for slavery that evolved in the South during the antebellum years and those that are made in defense of legalized abortion. Just before the Civil War, freed blacks such as Frederick Douglas were proving that given education and opportunity, the black man was the equal of the white in every way. Arguments in defense of slavery that had made of the black man less than a full person became increasingly absurd so that defenders of the institution were forced to move away from the issue of personhood to find new grounds for their position. If you have been following the last few years in the abortion debate, you will have noted the same kind of development. The latest arguments concentrate on "justifiable homicide." Simply stated, it is not that an unborn baby is not a person — there is too much evidence to the contrary — it is just that we can find reasons for killing someone with impunity. Justice Blackmun's decision looks fairly innocent in the face of this new kind of reasoning, though history has shown that his philosophy led us by a straight, unavoidable path to this outcome. Once you abandon the person, anything is possible.

Taney and Blackmun: An Unemotional Decision

At the time of the Dred Scott case, radical abolitionists and zealous Southern slave owners were ripping the country apart. In the microcosm of the nine-member Supreme Court, the same regional tensions and prejudices were at play. During the deliberations following the hearing of the Dred Scott case, the justices were wildly shouting at each other and waving their hands. Justice Taney took command of them with the words, "Brothers, this is the Supreme Court of the United States. Take your seats." Taney had no intention of allowing sentiment to govern the decision of the court. He insisted on remaining within the confines of Constitutional law and precedent. This was to be an unemotional, calculated, reasoned decision. His attitude would be perfectly mirrored in the 1973 Roe v. Wade deliberations. In Justice Harry Blackmun's words, the court wanted "to resolve the issue by constitutional measurement, free of emotion and of predilection."[74]

On the face of it, one would be glad that feelings are kept out of court deliberations. On the other hand, at a certain level and in a certain kind of discussion, one would not only expect strong feeling, but demand it. Feelings by themselves are irrational, but in proper order they serve to encourage good intentions and warn against evil. Our culture has falsely convinced us that real men do not cry. Real men do cry — they know when and for what to cry, when and for what to feel righteous anger.

Lincoln knew when to be angry. He had to deal frequently with people who encouraged the Civil War because they would be able to profit from it personally. One need only remember the vile words he had for Joseph Howard and Francis Mallison to appreciate the "rigid lack of compassion" that can accompany a man of noble principles. These two men were the newspaper workers that ran the false story of the military draft in order to make a killing in the gold market. The President had plenty of wrath and no mercy for such greed.

He was also famous for the swift disciplining of any officers who were "playing games with the war" by their public declarations to avoid battle and wait for it all to peter out. The John Key incident is a case in point. Following the battle of Antietam there were many voices claiming that the Union, despite grave losses, had failed to turn a stalemate into a decisive victory by not pursuing the retreating Confederates. Major John Key, an influential officer under General McClellan, wrote a report on the battle stating that the Union did not "bag" the Confederates because this was not the game. The plan was that both armies should be kept in the field until they were exhausted and a compromise would be reached on slavery. Lincoln responded

---

74. *Roe v. Wade*, 410 U.S. 113 (1973), opening remarks

speedily to this report and personally saw to it that Key was court-martialed. If there were any Northern officers who were losing battles, or purposely not winning them, Lincoln made it clear "it was his object to break up the game."

Lincoln's occasional fits of anger may have been politically insensitive but they were also politically necessary. Surrounded as he was by so many who just did not get the point, he had to resort at times to extreme action to break through their self-interest and clarify matters.

As a young man, Lincoln had considered the passions a danger to personal happiness and social peace. He had once hoped for the triumph of "cold, calculating reason" understood to mean a strict adherence to the American legal system. Yet, he could not, like Douglas, argue that since the Constitution did not outlaw slavery, it was to be permitted and allowed to expand. The injustice of slavery came smack up against his unqualified faith in the Constitution. After Dred Scott, he could never again view that document as the sole authority in the matter. As he grew to perceive more and more the ugliness of slavery, and to grasp the existence of an authority higher than the Constitution, he could not prevent the gradual integration of his head and his heart. Reason, feeling and will met in that moment when he stepped from moderate to leader and issued the Emancipation Proclamation.

The Burger Court believed that it was taking a neutral position when it heard Roe v. Wade. But since the case concerned a matter of life and death, neutrality was not possible. Matters of absolute truth often are made up of the stuff of life or death situations. One might be able to take a neutral position while something is not in motion, but not while a battle is waging. General McClellan sat with his army outside of Richmond; he took a neutral position in regards to the Confederacy. His inactivity, though highly frustrating to Lincoln, was not grounds for court martial — but it did nothing to end the war. He was simply useless. But should Lee have thrown his army at him and McClellan not responded — that would not have been neutrality — it would have been treason. When an army is on the march, you can either capitulate or fight. You cannot pretend nothing is happening. The tiny life in the womb is like an army on the march, only not as a threat but as a sign of hope and renewed energy. It is the march of life. One cannot be neutral about it.

Maybe our minds are too clouded by years of debate on this subject. Let's look at neutrality another way.

Suppose a research scientist claimed to have isolated a particular lab-created bacteria that would cure cancer. He has frozen it in storage in his laboratory. While it rests in this non-moving position, that is to say, neither being developed into an administrable drug nor harmed in any way, no action need be taken. But what if the bacteria are removed from their frozen condition and have only twenty-four hours to live? Let us imagine that the man who discovered the bacteria has died leaving instructions for some other scientist to successfully complete his work. No one in medical research could take a neutral position on such a matter. They would have to declare their belief in the drug and continue with the experiment, or declare their disbelief and let the bacteria die. Some might hold that a third option, to do nothing, was a choice in itself, but it does not take much to see that it amounts to the same as choice number two. In both instances, the bacteria are lost and cancer continues to be a modern plague.

Perhaps this example can get through to us because it has something to do with our good. There's something in it for us. Human nature is such that we don't get really riled up about something if we don't see it having any immediate affect on us. This was true of the Missouri Compromise in 1820, which prevented the extension of slavery. In point of fact, the Missouri Compromise didn't get much attention either by way of abrogation or criticism. There were simply not that many people out yonder across the big Mississippi for the people back east to care much about it. The frontier was another world. It was all so far away and unrealistic. Who cared if frontier folk had slaves or not? In short, a classic case of "out of sight, out of mind." Participation in the slavery debate grew in direct proportion to the increase in population in frontier territories as people in the east felt personally engaged by what was happening to their relatives on the frontier.

Maybe Americans can remain neutral about abortion because they do not see how each individual human life does something good for them. In this sense, each new life is an undiscovered frontier that seems too far away from our immediate and familiar world. Abortion doesn't threaten what we know and love, so why should we worry about it? What Americans don't realize is that we are all vitally involved with the fate of the unborn since the child's right to life, protected by our laws and our courts, means our own safety. The philosophy behind *Roe v. Wade* that allowed the termination of innocent human life in the name of privacy is a slippery slope. Pushed to its extreme, no one is indispensable. But, as long as Americans do not see their own personal danger involved in the issue of the unborn's right to life, a neutral position will seem possible.

There have been attempts to drive home the message. Historians have had some impact on the pro-choice mind set with their comparison between the fall of the Roman Empire and the steady moral decay of American society — but those who are not students of history can dismiss this argument as just idle speculation. What percentage of grade school and high school students today truly understand that those who fail to learn from history's errors are doomed to repeat them? Religions may appeal to God's laws, but in an agnostic society such an appeal reaches only a few. People are uncomfortable with teachings that emphasize personal responsibility, not to mention the pains of hell awaiting those on the forefront of the pro-choice movement. When Bishop Vaughn of New York expressed his doubts about the salvation of many pro-choice civil and government leaders, he was roundly criticized. Nor did he find support from his confreres in the episcopate. The lack of unity among his brother bishops made

Bishop Vaughn's prophetic comments slight indeed. But the fact is that such comments do cause many people to reconsider their stand on abortion.

Moderate pro-lifers remain confident that the "American way" will work things out in due season. They stay out of the direct fight and let different opinions reign where they will, hoping a harmony will be achieved on its own. It took a Civil War for the nation to come to its senses about slavery. Those who would sit on the fence about abortion must realize that they are in all likelihood condemning this nation to a conflict greater than any we have seen before.

Twenty-eight years have passed since the passage of *Roe v. Wade*. Forty million brutal deaths. If we react with horror and loathing to abortion — if we feel ourselves ready to cry out in protest — are we to suspend our feelings because they have no right to influence the political realm? If our laws allow legalized abortion, does that mean that we should convince ourselves not to feel what we feel? If we feel repelled by pictures of aborted fetuses, should we translate that reaction into condemnation of pro-lifers who are trying to open our eyes? What about the sadness and guilt from previous sexual encounters that ended or could have ended with abortion? Can we not admit that something right and natural moves in us when we feel regret for an abuse of our sexuality or remorse for a human life terminated in the womb? Should we short-circuit our feelings at the level of action? Are not our feelings in these matters more than mere sentiment, but right reason? If we fail to respond to these feelings, can we live with ourselves?

A Constitutional Faith

"That which is not just is not law"

William Lloyd Garrison

For a people enamored of the law, Americans for the most part practice a blind faith when it comes to their legal system. Such a legalistic mindset is supposed to guarantee harmony in society; but, on the contrary, as scripture says, "The law kills, while spirit gives life." Without a reference point above and beyond the written word of our Constitution and the various laws passed by our legislatures, we are doomed to fall into the same kind of injustice that kept Dred Scott a slave. We cannot be led by law alone.

Let me put things more concretely.

Human laws — that is, the laws passed by legislative authorities — have no say over the laws of physics which are prior to, or at least more fundamental, than man-made laws. For example, governments can dictate that airplanes shall not fly over homes at 100 feet or carry excessive loads; but no government body can decree that airplanes will always remain safely in the air until landing. Physical laws at work in airplane flight must be respected, and if for some reason they are violated or ignored, the airplane in question will be headed earthward. Clearly, then, in the physical world we are subject to laws outside of the Constitution. Such laws really do exist and we must acknowledge them if we want to live long, happy lives.

Human beings cannot free themselves from the laws of physics by thinking or dreaming themselves free. When we speak of freedom, we must remain within the boundaries of the possible and the impossible. A person in jail is free to think about a walk in the park all he wants, but since the iron bars prevent his body from going anywhere, he has to stay put. You can imagine yourself able to fly off the highest cliff and soar like a bird, but as long as this idea remains only an idea, you are not in danger. If you should take a real bodily leap off a cliff, you will answer to the laws of nature. To use another example, one can dream all day long about having a baby, but conception will not occur until the will directs the body in a certain way with the body of another.

All of this seems pretty clear on the physical level. What we must accept is that man is bound by another set of laws that are not physical but just as insistent. To violate these laws is comparable to taking a free dive off a cliff. Yet, oddly enough, as soon as we start talking about these less visible laws the discussion is placed on the level of "religion" and therefore considered outside the proper consideration of legislatures and courts.

We are a people without metaphysics. The prefix "meta" comes from the Greek word meaning "above." To have some kind of metaphysical system means to see above and beyond that which presents itself to our eyes and ears and acknowledge realities that cannot be seen in a physical way. Concepts such as beauty, goodness, and truth fall into this category. Human nature does, as well. Throughout the history of Christendom, up to modern times, these invisibles were taken for granted as much as physical phenomena. Their existence was not a relativistic religious issue since it was considered to be a function of simple human reason to postulate the existence of things not seen.

Human laws cannot ignore the metaphysical nature of man.

When they do, justice is not their aim since justice is itself a metaphysical concept.

Let's consider how the lack of metaphysics affected the *Dred Scott v. Sandford* case.

Chief Justice Roger Brooke Taney was recognized as "a first-rate legal mind," and "a clear, forceful writer" who "realized that constitutional law required vision and common sense as well as careful legal analysis . . . to find in the United States Constitution the necessary authority for states to solve their own problems

. . ."[75] He considered himself an exemplar of fidelity to the Constitution since he put the law above everything else, even if it offended his moral judgement. When Taney reviewed Dred Scott's case, it was under the illumination of one source and one source only — the Constitution as it was written on plain paper.

Justice Taney was only representative of his time. Those who wanted to avoid controversy and forestall imminent conflict on the question of slavery sought shelter under the wings of the Constitution. And who was entrusted with interpreting the Constitution? The Supreme Court. No one need worry himself or herself any further once the Court had spoken. This belief extended downward from the highest office in the land. A few moments after being sworn into office by Chief Justice Taney, President Buchanan indicated the confidence he placed in the Supreme Court to resolve the matter: "Slavery . . . is a judicial question which . . .belongs to the Supreme Court of the United States, before whom it . . . will . . .be speedily and finally settled. To their decision, I shall cheerfully submit whatever this may be . . ."[76]

The Supreme Court, then, would serve as the mouthpiece of the Constitution, repeating only what it heard with literal exactness. When Taney came to write his decision for Dred Scott, he expressed the limits that he placed on the Court's activity:

> **"It is not the province of the Court to decide upon the justice or injustice, the policy or impolicy of these laws. The decision of that question belonged to the political or lawmaking power; to those who . . . framed the Constitution. The duty of the Court**

---

75. William H. Rehnquist, *The Supreme Court. How it Was, How It Is* (New York, NY: William Morrow, 1987), p. 150
76. *Inaugural Addresses of the Presidents of the United States from George Washington 1789 to Richard Milhous Nixon 1969* (Washington, D.C.: United States Government Printing Office, 1969), p. 112 (James Buchanan's Inaugural Address, March 4, 1857)

*is to interpret the instrument they have framed . . .
according to its true intent and meaning when it
was adopted.* "[77]

One has to ponder what Taney had in mind when he said, "the
true intent and meaning." He certainly was not referring to any
abstract notions of justice, equality and freedom that the Founding
Fathers may have had. He remained strictly intra-textual in his
interpretation of the Constitution. He proved this by saying, " . . .
there are two clauses in the Constitution which point . . . directly to
the Negro race as a separate class of persons, and show clearly that
they were not regarded as . . . citizens of the government then
formed . . . it is obvious that they were not even in the minds of the
framers of the Constitution when they were conferring special
rights and privileges upon the citizens of a state in every other part
of the Union."[78]

And there we have it. The only light Taney was reading under
was the reflexive light of a written document. He stretched his hand
nowhere further for assistance to judge the case before him. He
looked at a black man. He looked at the Constitution. He looked
back at the black man and saw property.

How many Americans realize that the exact same argument
was made in *Roe v. Wade*? And if they realize it, are they moved
with the disgust that such a rigidly legal frame of mind should
provoke?

Following the second round of hearings on *Roe v. Wade*, Chief
Justice Burger asked Justice Harry Blackmun to pen the court's
decision. Blackmun had done copious research on the history of
abortion and abortion law. He inserted this as the backdrop for the
decision, but in the actual determination of the case he did exactly
what Taney had done — he went to the Constitution to find the
definition of "person." In an eerie echo of the past Blackmun

---

77. *Dred Scott v. Sandford*, 19 Howard 393 (1857)
78. *Ibid*

writes, "The Constitution does not define "person" in so many words. Section I of the Fourteenth Amendment contains three references to "person." The first, in defining "citizens," speaks of "persons born or naturalized in the United States." The word also appears both in the Due Process Clause and in the Equal Protection Clause. "Person" is used in other places in the Constitution . . . But in nearly all these instances, the use of the word is such that it has application only post-natally. None indicates, with any assurance, that it has any possible prenatal application."[79]

One can see that this decision is rooted in a prejudice as profound as that of Roger Brooke Taney's prejudice against African-Americans. Prior to this decision, another decision had already been made. It's like Hamlet asking, "To be or not to be." You can only ask that question if you have already decided life has little meaning. Even before Justice Taney heard Dred Scott's case, he had already assigned the African-American a sub-human role. In the same way, before he heard the proceedings of *Roe v. Wade*, Justice Blackmun held the *a priori* opinion that an unborn child is not a person. The Constitution merely gave him the means for writing his prejudice into the Court's opinion.

Regardless of pre-existing prejudices, all judges can be challenged by the cases before them to re-examine their opinions in light of justice and the good of the society they serve. This could have happened for both Taney and Blackmun, but instead they chose to hide behind written words on an old page of parchment, incensed religiously with a smoke screen of rhetoric. One could say that both justices suffered from a disproportionate affection and attachment to the Constitution inspired by a personal or professional fear of facing the truth.

Unfortunately, many Americans today share the same creed. They wrap themselves in the security blanket of the Constitution believing that the wisdom of that document is so good it contains

---

79. *Roe v. Wade*, 410 U.S. 113 (1973), Section IX.A

within itself every cure for society's problems. They may not like abortion, but in the name of the personal freedoms they believe to be spelled out in the Constitution, they will allow it to exist. It is much the same kind of thinking with pornography. Better to allow the bad and the good together than to risk losing our freedom of speech. If we wish to be a nation in which freedom of the press is protected, we must allow many different kinds of things to be said. We must give a floor to all kinds of hatred — the Ku Klux Klan, for example. This argument is currently being used in defense of pornographic and hate-oriented websites — new platforms for an old debate.

We Americans have always believed that our laws somehow captured the higher principles of truth and justice so often lacking in other governments. We have believed ourselves to be a beacon of light and hope to the world. Justice Blackmun's decision had the drastic effect of blowing that light out. We are no longer different from the rest. Those who were liberated from oppression are now the oppressors. This is what inevitably happens when mankind claims for itself the highest authority in the making of laws, instead of seeking a standard that is somehow above or outside purely man made reality. Roe v. Wade was not just destructive of human life; it disrupted the harmony that must exist between natural and human law. In his philosophically charged opinion, Blackmun established much more than the right to legalized abortion. He put the seal of approval on the detachment of American law from natural law. Thus, we have become like gods, the sole arbitrators of good and evil.

The point is that once the fundamental notion of person is lost, everything becomes a play of semantics. It is easy to get caught up in the intellectual roller-coaster ride — we all have a certain fascination with puzzles. But the intricacy of an argument can never escape the verity or falsehood of its fundamental premise. The fundamental premise in Roe v. Wade is that somehow human beings may live free of the powers of nature. I refer here not merely to a physical nature which allows for human procreation, but also to the love of truth, justice, and the good which is part and parcel of being human. Somehow, the court was able to close its eyes to a great many truths about the human being and, if you will, "re-invent" us. By our government's insistence on maintaining *Roe v. Wade* these past twenty-eight years, we have enshrined at the heart of our society the conviction that ideas are higher than realities, that fantasy is truer than fact, and that our intellectual achievements are superior and can operate independently of the natural world around us and within us.

There was a time when even a twelve-year-old would have laughed at the notion that we have the power to disregard the laws of nature. Since the sexual revolution of the sixties, we have lived like a people "above the law" — the laws of nature, that is. Now, young people are more apt to make the commercial slogan, "Just do it," the philosophical principle upon which to live. What has been the result? We have only to consider the terrifying proliferation of venereal disease and AIDS and the dismal failure of sex education to curb teen pregnancy. Too many have discovered too late that years of hormone pills leads to sterility or breast cancer. The facts are in, and they are forcing us to admit that we are not free to play with our sexuality anymore than we are to drive a car into a wall at 60 mph without some result. Such is the sorry state of affairs in a generation born and raised under the shadow of *Roe v. Wade*.

Shadows

The so-called Constitutional "right of privacy" upon which the *Roe v. Wade* decision is based comes from a "reading between the lines" of the Bill of Rights and the implications of the Ninth and Fourteenth Amendments to the Constitution. The groundwork for a "right of privacy" had been well laid long before Jane Roe set her case before the Court. Justice Blackmun was simply following a precedent established in certain previous Supreme Court rulings beginning with *Griswold v. Connecticut* in 1965. At that time, the Warren Court struck down a Connecticut law banning the distribution, use, etc., of contraceptives. Justice Douglas, writing the opinion for the case, described a constitutional "right of privacy," not stated but implied by the Bill of Rights and certain constitutional amendments, existing as a kind of penumbra, or shadow. Justices Black and Steward strongly disagreed, holding that a right not given in the Constitution cannot be called a "Constitutional right." Nevertheless, the notion of a right of privacy had been born and would see a rapid evolution.

In *Eisenstadt v. Baird* (1972) the court found another bit of leverage for the right of privacy. In response to a Massachusetts statute making it a crime for anyone to distribute contraceptives, other than doctors and pharmacists prescribing them to married people, the Burger court ruled that single women also have the right to acquire and use contraceptives. To deny them that right violated the Fourteenth Amendment's equal protection clause. In the decision penned by Justice Brennan, the right of privacy picked up strength as the Justice determined it to be something that inheres in the individual, not married couples. In the Justice's words, "If the right to privacy means anything, it is the right of the individual, married or single, to be free from unwarranted government intrusion into matters so fundamentally affecting a person as the decision whether to bear or beget a child."

It takes no great leap of intellect to see that the stage was being set for *Roe v. Wade*.

From the right of privacy, Justice Blackmun derived the fundamental right of women, single or married, to choose whether or not to carry to term the child within them. Simply stated, that meant whether or not to have an abortion. In Section V of the *Roe* decision, he states: "The principal thrust of appellant's attack on the Texas statutes is that they improperly invade a right, said to be possessed by the pregnant woman, to choose to terminate her pregnancy. Appellant would discover this right in the concept of personal "liberty" embodied in the Fourteenth Amendment's Due Process Clause; or in personal, marital, familial, and sexual privacy said to be protected by the Bill of Rights or its penumbras . . ." In Section VIII, Blackmun merely repeats this shaky argument, holding it up as the rock solid basis of his final decision: "This right of privacy whether it be founded in the Fourteenth Amendment's concept of personal liberty and restrictions upon state action, as we feel it is, or, as the District Court determined, in the Ninth Amendment's reservation of rights to the people, is broad enough to encompass a woman's decision whether or not to terminate her pregnancy . . . We therefore conclude that the right of personal privacy includes the abortion decision, but that this right is not unqualified and must be considered against important state interests in regulations."

From out of the shadows came legalized abortion — quite literally.

But this was not the first time that a shadow generated injustice in the American judicial system. Another kind of shadow hung over the Taney court that upheld slavery. At that time the court's prejudice created the shadow. Looking to the founding documents of the nation, the justices could not find the extension of "life, liberty and the pursuit of happiness" to the black man. Since they could not find the actual words, "The African-American is a person, possessing the same nature and equal dignity of the white man," they assumed that the Founding Fathers never intended the rights of American citizenship for the African who had been transported to this country in bondage. In both cases, the Taney and Burger courts were dealing with intangibles, and found themselves woefully inadequate to the task at hand.

Let us give Justice Blackmun the benefit of the doubt and allow that he felt he had to protect freedom by allowing for the widest interpretation of the Ninth Amendment possible. He probably saw himself as a great crusader for freedom — a true progressive in the annihilation of social evil. In his own mind he probably had the status of a Frederick Douglas or a Susan B. Anthony and, like them, he was willing to take the heat for his bold move forward in personal liberty. He could relish in these notions because in his mind "law" only meant Constitutional law. We could paraphrase Martin Luther, "Here I stand on the Constitution; the Constitution and the Constitution alone is the sole source of authority in my life. If you cannot show me in the Constitution where abortion is outlawed, then I can do nothing."

Nearly a century and a half ago, Chief Justice Taney felt much the same way about his court's decision. He never regretted or repented of his decision in *Dred Scott*. "I have an abiding confidence that this act of my judicial life will stand the test of time and the sober judgement of the country."[80] In his own mind he was opposed to slavery, but by virtue of his office he was sworn to uphold the Constitution as he saw it — but because he didn't see any definition of person he had to make one up. Believing himself to be pure of ulterior motives, as well as faithful to the framers of the Constitution, Taney felt martyred by the public outcry against his decision in *Dred Scott v. Sandford*: "At my time of life when my end must be near, I should have rejoiced to find that the irritating strifes of this world were over, and that I was about to depart in peace with all men . . . "[81]

A Person - When the Law Says So?

Did African-Americans become persons because the Thirteenth Amendment said so? Clearly not. Does the unborn child become a person when the Supreme Court says so? We know that despite the legal gymnastics involved in defining a constitutional right to privacy, the question of personhood is the only relevant question.

Justice Blackmun himself acknowledged, "The appellee and

---

80. Letter of Roger Brooke Taney to President Franklin Pierce, August 29, 1857, quoted in *Roger B. Taney* by Carl Brent Swisher (New York, NY: The Macmillan Company, 1935), pp. 518-519
81. *Ibid*

certain amici argue that the fetus is a 'person' within the language and meaning of the Fourteenth Amendment. In support of this, they outline at length and in detail the well-known facts of fetal development. If this suggestion of personhood is established, the appellant's case, of course, collapses for the fetus' right to life would then be guaranteed specifically by the Amendment."[82] Yet, although Blackmun acknowledges the priority of the argument, he is unable to take the positive step of stating what his own heart must tell him: the unborn child is a human person. He makes but a passing reference to the possibility of the child's personhood when he writes of the state's interest in abortion: Blackman continues: "The third reason is the state's interest — some phrase it in terms of duty in protecting prenatal life. **Some** of the argument for this justification rests on the theory that a new human life is present from the moment of conception."[83]

Some? Good Lord! Everything rests on this point, yet the Justice relegates it to one consideration among many. This is a little like a judge trying a robbery case, telling the lawyer for the accused robber, "Some of your argument, Sir, depends on the determination that money was indeed stolen." Or, could you imagine a judge continuing a murder trial after the alleged murder victim walks into the room? The defense lawyer stand up, "See your honor, my client could not have killed Mr. Smith, as you can see he is quite alive." Then the judge strokes his chin and says, "Some of your arguments would seem to depend on this fact. We better take a recess to think things over." Everything about the legality of abortion should depend on the question: Is the fetus a person? But Blackmun's casual reference to "some of the argument" reveals that in actuality, the person is not the central issue at all. This being clear, one can see that Roe v. Wade blows the political field wide open. No one and nothing can be safe anymore.

82. *Roe v. Wade*, 410 U.S. 113 (1973), Section IX.A.
83. *Roe v. Wade*, 410 U.S. 113 (1973), Section VII.5

How did the issue of personhood get lost?

Imagine an accountant who was so totally engrossed in his profession that he always gave his wife a print out version of their financial picture for their wedding anniversary. No matter how hard you tried to convince him, he could not think of anything else to give her. Debits and credits defined everything in his life. Or imagine a corporate contract lawyer who is so single-mindedly engrossed in his work that he cannot even discuss a potential trip to the zoo with his nine-year-old son without first drawing up the appropriate contractual papers. Church professionals, too, are subject to this kind of myopia. Ministers, for instance, who are so concerned with applying every suggestion from their latest workshop that they actually issue detailed instructions forbidding children from carrying rosaries in their hands as they walk up to receive First Holy Communion. Many church theologians are so engrossed in the academic research and the approval of their peers that they never look outside long enough to see how little positive results these works are having in pews on Sunday mornings.

Justice Henry Blackmun was a lawyer. He threw himself totally into his profession and specialized in constitutional law. What happened next is probably an occupational hazard. He began to perceive reality through the lens of his legal training. He squeezed all of it into a tiny porthole. The United States Constitution became not just a great document that helped establish a new country, it became the creed of his religion. Blackmun is like a man who thinks he can move a grand piano into his living room because he has just put down new tiles. When the floor collapses he will realize that it is not the tiles but the basement support which needs attention. Or, we can compare him to a man who leaps out of a boat and lands on a rock. He calls to his companions to follow and then watches them drown. If only he had realized that the little rock upon which he stood was not sufficient ground for everyone else.

But Blackmun's moment of truth arrived. He was presented with a difficult question: Is a human fetus a human being? He stroked his chin, cracked his knuckles, wiped his brow, paced back and forth and panicked. The concept of "being" was quite foreign to him. It wasn't part of his academic preparation. To answer the question he had only one source, the Constitution. With confidence he rushed to the shelf and took out his copy and found the closest thing to the term "human being" that he could find: "person." He breathed a sigh of relief, since he had dealt with "person" before. Such a concept had even been applied to companies. So he looked at how the word "person" was used in law. To his bitter disappointment, none of these texts dealt with abortion. He concluded: the Founding Fathers said nothing about it, therefore, I must be silent on the matter."

When Justice Harry Blackmun circulated his draft of the *Roe v. Wade* decision, he told everyone, "It has been an interesting assignment." What kind of interest did he find in it? Perhaps it was the historical research that he did on the history of abortion and its place in the law. That he was proud of his work is evident. In an unprecedented move, he prepared a special statement to be read from the bench when announcing the Court's decision and had copies made and circulated to reporters. Usually, reporters received only the text of the decision. However, Blackmun felt the need to make it very clear that the Texas abortion laws which the Court were striking down were an infringement on a woman's constitutional right of privacy.

Why did the Justice have to make the matter so clear? Because he could see the weakness of his own argument and knew it must be supported by something else. He reaches — what a stretch! — for the right of privacy. If the fetus is truly not a person, then Justice Blackmun's thinking makes all the sense in the world. If the fetus is a person, than he becomes one of history's greatest tyrants giving the greatest power — that of life and death — to those who can exercise it over the poorest and weakest of all.

American Chicken Pie

An amazing characteristic of the Roe v. Wade decision as penned by Blackmun is the Justice's belief that no real consensus exists about the beginning of human life while at the same time presenting a detailed history of opinions on all aspects of the question. How can Blackmun acknowledge so many great thinkers, philosophers, religious denominations and legal authorities, and yet be unsatisfied that at least a doubt exists on when human life begins?

I like to call this the "American Chicken Pie Principle." This is quite different from any "apple pie principle" you may be familiar with. The "American Chicken Pie Principle," roughly stated, asserts that "I will make no stand, or declare no truth, so long as there exist various opinions on the matter." This principle is closely aligned with a special brand of American schizophrenia in which one deathly fears being controversial while at the same time feeling oneself drawn to controversy. The evidence for the malady is the number of viewers for shows such as Jerry Springer or 60 Minutes. A universal principle of journalism and media producers springs from the knowledge that "controversy sells."

Justice Henry Blackmun displayed the fullness of the American chicken pie syndrome in his dismissal of the Hippocratic Oath. For centuries, all doctors were subject to this oath which bound them to the service of life. In it was included a condemnation of procured abortion. Blackmun's opinion, working from an interpretation by a Dr. Edelstein, states: "The Oath was not uncontested even in Hippocrates' day . . . Most Greek thinkers . . . commended abortion, at least prior to viability . . . For the Pythagoreans, however, it was a matter of dogma. For them the embryo was animate from the moment of conception, and abortion meant destruction of a living being. The abortion clause of the Oath, therefore, 'echoes Pythagorean doctrines,' and '[I]n no other stratum of Greek opinion were such views held or proposed in the same spirit of uncompromising austerity.' "[84]

---

84. *Roe v. Wade*, 410 U.S. 113 (1973), Section VI.2

Justice Blackmun neglects to consider the fact that the longevity of the Hippocratic Oath has won for it a sense of authority. He discredits the witness of 2000 years of history in favor of that eras contemporary diverse opinions. He is correct in asserting that other opinions existed at the time the Hippocratic Oath was first designed, but he fails to note that the Oath, not these circulating opinions, won the universal and perennial assent of mankind. Few Greek names are recognized as readily as is Hippocrates. Might it just be that of many diverse opinions, some are right and others wrong? Perhaps the Hippocratic Oath existed for so long because it contained certain fundamental truths recognizable to all men of all times.

In his historical account of abortion, Justice Blackmun picks and chooses from the record what he needs to justify the Court's decision. He focuses on the question of quickening — the first recognizable movement of the fetus in utero — as an example of the wide disagreement among scholars on the precise moment when human life begins. For every voice he can find who claimed abortion after quickening is murder, he drums up another voice which held the contrary.

Justice Blackmun dismisses not only the wisdom of many ancient philosopher-doctors, he also casts aside the opinion of the American Medical Association claiming it was only a reflection of the "anti-abortion mood prevalent in this country in the late 19th century." In 1871 the AMA's Committee on Criminal Abortion had explained their condemnation of abortion by saying, "We had to deal in human life. In a matter of less importance we could entertain no compromise. An honest judge on the bench would call things by their proper names. We could do no less . . . we call the attention of the clergy of all denominations to the perverted views of morality entertained by a large class of females — aye, and men also, on this important issue."[85] Lucky for Blackmun, he can then skip ahead a hundred years to show how much the AMA has changed its tune. As Blackmun describes it, the AMA's fall from

---

85. *Roe v. Wade*, 410 U.S. 113 (1973), Section VI.6

grace shows the American chicken pie principle at work again: "In 1970, after the introduction of a variety of proposed resolutions, and of a report from its Board of Trustees, a reference committee noted 'polarization of the medical profession on this controversial issue'; division among those who had testified; a difference of opinion among AMA councils and committees; 'the remarkable shift in testimony' in six months, felt to be influenced 'by rapid changes in state laws and by the judicial decisions which tend to make abortion more freely available'; and a feeling 'that this trend will continue.' "[86]

As for the religious/philosophical field, here is just a sampling of the ingredients Blackmun whipped together for his American chicken pie:

It should be sufficient to note briefly the wide divergence of thinking on this most sensitive and difficult question. There has always been strong support for the view that life does not begin until live birth. This was the belief of the Stoics . . . the predominant, though not the unanimous attitude of the Jewish faith . . . a large segment of the Protestant community . . . organized groups that have taken a formal position on the abortion issue have generally regarded abortion as a matter for the conscience of the individual and her family . . . common law found greater significance in quickening. Physicians . . . have tended to focus either upon conception, upon live birth, or upon the interim point at which the fetus becomes "viable" . . . The Aristotelian theory of "mediate animation," that held sway through the Middle Ages and the Renaissance in Europe, continued to be official Roman Catholic dogma until the 19th century, despite opposition to this "ensoulment" theory from

---

86. *Roe v. Wade*, 410 U.S. 113 (1973), Section VI.6

*those in the Church who would recognize the
existence of life from the moment of conception.
The latter is now, of course, the official belief of the
Catholic Church . . . a view strongly held by many
non-Catholics as well, and by many physicians.*[87]

Blackmun certainly did his research, but cleary the authority of religious denominations had little weight for him. Perhaps he did not even realize the implications of his own examples. First he says, "It [the opinion that life begins at birth] may be taken to represent also the position of a large segment of the Protestant community, in so far as that can be ascertained . . . " Then he asserts the clear-cut belief of the Catholic Church in "the existence of life from the moment of conception." While recognizing that Protestantism does not teach anything definitively on the subject of abortion, he admits that the Catholic Church does. But the authority of a 2000-year-old institution whose membership includes millions does not cause Blackmun to place even the shadow of a doubt on the question of when life begins. His argument is this: since I can find different religions saying different things, there is no answer to the question.

Blackmun is like a silly man trapped in a burning building. He knows he needs a rope to get to safety, but he refuses those who are throwing him a rope because there are others who are saying that it is not really a rope they are throwing him, it is something else, and they can't be trusted. In this situation, we can say there are only two positions: a) It really is a rope and the person throwing it to you can be trusted, or b) it is not a rope and you cannot trust the person throwing it. To imagine there is a third position — the neutral position — is absurd. If the house is burning down, you need a rope to get out. The pessimist and the moderate will both end up roasted.

Given the cafeteria-style serving of information that

---

87. *Roe v. Wade*, 410 U.S. 113 (1973), Section IX.B

Blackmun has gathered as a backdrop to the Court's decision, he concludes, "We need not resolve the difficult question of when life begins. When those trained in the respective disciplines of medicine, philosophy, and theology are unable to arrive at any consensus, the judiciary at this point in the development of man's knowledge, is not in a position to speculate as to the answer."[88]

What a sad moment! Not only for the millions of unborn children who will die as a result of *Roe v. Wade*, but for all Americans who will watch the unfolding of this flawed philosophical position. With this statement, Blackmun separates the law profession from the community of freethinking intellectuals. Lawyers and judges are, in his opinion, not to incorporate philosophical ideas into their mental faculties. They must only make calculated deductions from what is given to them in the law. What Blackmun did not want to recognize is the fact that there are many "trained in the respective disciplines of medicine, philosophy and theology" who are quite able to give a clear answer to the question of when human life begins. That he personally was not convinced such proofs exist says more about his own mental and moral make-up than it does about the value of the arguments. He embodies in a frightening way the corrupt side of the Scribes and Pharisees with whom Jesus had to deal. The Pharises looked at their scriptures and saw nothing that said "God will become a man." So they concluded God cannot become a man. Jesus tried to overcome their hardness of heart with the sharp sword of truth and the gentle persuasion of love.

An Unrestricted Restriction

One of the rationalizations Justice Blackmun used in his decision to legalize abortion was the reassuring statement that he was not prohibiting all forms of restrictions on abortions. The

---

88. *Roe v. Wade*, 410 U.S. 113 (1973), Section IX.B

specific parameter of Roe v. Wade was to be the first trimester of pregnancy. The court gave freedom to the states, if they wanted it, to regulate later abortions. This was due, he noted, to a justifiable interest of the state in unborn human life.

This aspect of the court's decision presents us with an example of bad logic and bad policy. It embodies a fatal flaw. In effect, the court gave the freedom to legislative bodies to restrict abortion while at the same time refusing to lay down restrictions itself. Blackmun accepts an incredibly naïve assumption about law and order: that a lower authority will be able to make restrictions on certain freedoms where a higher authority refuses to do so. The practical consequence of this flawed thinking is easy to figure out. Those who sense their freedom is taken away by a law made by a lower authority will, as sure as the sun rises, appeal to the higher authority that has already made clear its intention to protect that freedom. The historical evidence for all this is to be found in the wake of *Roe v. Wade*. Every restriction on abortion passed by the states was challenged in court, sending case after case careening towards the highest court in the land which, in its turn, no longer wished to adjudicate the subject.

Let us give Justice Blackmun the benefit of the doubt again. Perhaps he forgot that his was the highest court in the land. On the other hand, Justice Blackmun was an intelligent man and could not have failed to appreciate that the constitutional right to abortion he and his confreres had maintained would undo all efforts on the lower levels of government. Let me put it this way: Blackmun's decision is something akin to a boss's decision to fire an employee. The employee may protest and challenge the boss and threaten to take the matter up with the other employees, but the boss knows very well that no matter how much of a raucous the man causes, the opinions of his employees mean nothing to his decision. He is the boss, and his word is final. Unless the employee can find another authority to challenge the authority of his boss, the employee is sunk.

Blackmun agrees that there should be restrictions. He is saying, "I think hospitals should be safe." This is like Jefferson Davis saying, "I think slaves should be treated nicely." If that seems silly, we can understand just how worthless and irresponsible is Blackmun's opinion. Stating that he believes in restrictions to abortions after establishing the philosophical grounds to justify every kind of abortion imaginable . . . This is like leaving a group of children alone in a knife factory and saying, "Now, don't hurt anyone." Knowing the nature of children prohibits the responsible person from taking such an action or making such a statement. Just as a slave owner will beat his slaves to get more work out of them, a sexually promiscuous society will only decrease restrictions on abortion, not put more in place.

I would like to point out another example in American political life that illustrates the need to solve problems with due regard to the nature of human beings. Let us consider the universal desire of people for good health care. It would be an incredibly naïve politician who proposed this solution to our current crisis: "We will settle the problem of the high cost of health care by passing a law stating that hospitals are now free to restrict the salaries of their workers. We will also pass a law that allows doctors and nurses to work half of their hours for no pay." Such a proposal might be considered idealistic — but more likely it would just be considered silly.

The point of this illustration is not to divert to a discussion of health care, but to see how a naïve view of human nature leads to poor legislation. If we had a nation of citizens as selfless as St. Francis or Mother Theresa we could get away with it. But let's face the music. No law is needed to allow people to work for free if they want to. I don't think many bosses would protest and demand that one be forcibly restrained from such a generous act done in the interest of saving the hospital's financial life and the good of patients. For Lincoln, the hope that slave owners would voluntarily free the slaves was just such a naïve idea. One of his great insights into human nature was, "The Autocrat of all Russians will resign his crown, and proclaim his subjects free republicans sooner than will our American masters voluntarily give up their slaves."[89]

But here again is precisely what Judge Blackmun has done in regard to his "deep concerns" that abortion should be restricted by the states in some cases. He fails to see that if one needs an abortion in the early stages of pregnancy, that need is not going to change simply because a woman is now at a later stage in the pregnancy. *Doe v. Bolton*, the companion case to *Roe v. Wade*, proved the slippery slope nature of Justice Blackmun's philosophical premise by opening the door to abortion without restrictions beyond the first trimester. Partial birth abortion is the logical and inevitable outcome of the principles Blackmun used to defend *Roe v. Wade*.

Consider well the incredible parallels between the battle over the personhood of the African-American and the present fight regarding the unborn child. Americans of the 1860's readily accepted the prejudicial opinions underlying the Taney Court's decision to declare a black man a piece of property. Incredibly, or perhaps not too incredibly, Americans today have grown comfortable with the philosophical assumptions behind *Roe v. Wade*. But the price of this disinterest in the value of human life is great. The time is already upon us when philosophical principles adopted by the Burger Court in 1973 are being extended to life at other stages. The safety of each person, born or unborn, is at stake.

Justice Blackmun's decision represented the most significant national teaching regarding the nature of the human person and the role of law since the Civil War. In essence, the Justice chose to ignore his experience, his feelings, his conscience, and every other quality of genuine humanity to find security in the dead letter of law. If he had only looked more to life and less to law. If he had only observed that every living thing grows from invisible beginnings into the fully matured creature right in front of our noses. If he had only applied this basic awareness to the human

---

89. Donald, *Lincoln*, p. 187

fetus which grows into a baby boy or girl. If he had only noticed that plant life only produces baby plants, animals baby animals, and human beings baby humans.

The moral of the story is that America survived her first great threat to national unity because she was able to rise above a Constitutional fideism to the "true liberty of the sons of God." Her human heart was re-awakened and the spirit of the law, not its letter, won the day. Eventually, the letter of the law would reflect that spirit.

Part III

Saving Graces

The Living and the Dead

The Constitution at the time of the Civil War stood in striking similarity to the Bible during the period of Reformation. Both the Confederates and the Northern "conservatives" held the Constitution to be the ultimate and only authority on matters of justice. They disagreed bitterly over its interpretation, but both continually resorted to it to solve the nation's conflict over slavery. Their approach was strictly literal. If it wasn't written in the Constitution, it wasn't up for consideration. One could say that politicians of the time acted in much the same way as Martin Luther who held up the Bible as the only authority to be recognized in matters of faith. The rallying cry for the Reformation was "sola scriptura!" ("only scripture!"). That left no room for interpretation; no reading of the "spirit of the law." If it wasn't actually written in the Bible, no definitive word could be pronounced.

Fortunately, this strict adherence to the law did not win out at the time of the Civil War. In fact, a close analysis of the spirit of the Northern position, in contrast to the spirit of the Confederacy, sheds light on the ultimate value of living tradition as opposed to "sola scriptura" for the survival and growth of a society. I would be so bold as to suggest that it was a particularly Catholic approach to American law that saved this nation at the time of the Civil War. This may seem an odd comparison to make. America is, after all, not a Catholic country. Not only were most of the early colonists Protestants, but the American temperament, forged on the frontier, embraced wholeheartedly the notion of personal freedom outweighing obedience to authority. Americans become indignant at the slightest suggestion of a rigid dogmatism that might stand in the way of an individual's right to realize his destiny. Each man is supposed to be self-determining, approaching life through the self-generated light of his own understanding. This conviction would seem to conflict with the popular notion of Catholicism.

Nonetheless, an analysis of the events that brought us through the Civil War reveal not only the importance of living tradition, but also the necessity of personal teaching authority as necessary safeguards of a people's faith and unity.

Catholicism has always held to the holy, sacred, and authoritative nature of the Bible as the written word of God. At the same time, however, what distinguishes Catholicism from other Christian denominations is her conviction that scripture requires the authoritative interpretation of a human being. Of course, those outside the faith misunderstand this teaching authority (called "Magisterium") to be a process of "inventing" doctrine. On the contrary, the Magisterium can only pass on what it has received. The Catholic Church stands on Christ's promise to St. Peter that on the person of Peter he would build his Church and the "gates of hell would not prevail against it." From the first Peter to the present day Pope in Rome extends an unbroken line of a living, breathing, teaching Magisterium. The fruit of this belief is the unity of faith that Catholics enjoy. Protestant tradition, on the other hand, recognizes no necessity for interpretation of scripture by any second party. Each individual conscience may, with the light of the Holy Spirit, understand scripture's intent. The practical outcome of this position was the almost immediate fracturing of the first Reformation assembly into other denominations as different individuals claimed a different understanding of scripture.

If "sola scriptura" had remained the battle cry of this country at the time of the Civil War, a similar splintering would have followed as each state went its own way. Fortunately, Abraham Lincoln, though American to the core and decidedly of a Protestant Christian inclination, did not hold the Constitution as sacrosanct. He was not tied to the letter of the law. He even had a remarkably "papal flair," if I may be allowed to say so, which sometimes brought down upon him the severe censure of his contemporaries. He was called an "autocrat" and a "tyrant." When he tried to persuade the Border States to voluntarily free some of their slaves, he received thousands of replies like this one from a

Kentucky congressman: "Confine yourself to your constitutional authority."[90]

Lincoln grew accustomed to such charges and didn't let himself be sidetracked by them. He knew that what he was doing was constitutional, if not according to the letter than certainly according to the spirit. We see this clearly in his response to Thaddeus Stevens, leader of the Pennsylvanian Republicans, who scolded Lincoln for enacting blockades of Southern ports. Stevens argued that such a move would give the world the idea the United States was recognizing the Confederacy as a nation. "We are blockading ourselves," complained Stevens. But Lincoln, a good lawyer himself, responded, "I don't know anything about the law of nations, and I thought it was all right. I'm a good enough lawyer in a Western law court, I suppose, but we didn't practice the law of nations back there . . ."[91] In other words, Lincoln was using the *dictates of his conscience* where the constitutional law he had studied was silent.

On another occasion, Erastus Corning attacked Lincoln for the exiling of Clement Vallandigham, the pro-slavery Northerner. Corning wrote that such treatment of Vallandigham was a "blow . . . against the spirit of our laws and Constitution" and an abrogation of "the liberty of speech and of the press, the right of trial by jury, the law of evidence, and the privilege of habeas corpus." Lincoln responded with remarkable affinity to a Catholic pontiff. Simply put, his answer was "I have spoken." Now, Catholics are familiar with the dictum, "Rome has spoken, the cause is decided," but such a notion of the authority of one man over the beliefs of others would send chills throughout the body of an American individualist's heart. However, this would only be the case if Lincoln (or the Pope, for that matter) was acting in a completely arbitrary way. Closer examination of Lincoln's action in the Vallandigham matter reveals that he did nothing to contradict the

90. Donald, *Lincoln*, p. 362
91. Donald, *Lincoln*, p. 303

Constitution and everything to protect it. He realized, even if his enemies refused to admit it, that the "Constitution itself provided for the suspension of these liberties, 'in cases of Rebellion or Invasion, or when the public safety may require it.' "[92]

Fortunately for the nation, Abraham Lincoln was a man firmly set in eternal truths which transcend the fragile passage of nation states and man-made constitutions. This elevated position gave him the freedom to trust his own conscience. He wasn't afraid of "imposing his morality" on anyone because he understood that morality is not a matter of opinion. Leaders should not need to take a poll on an issue to judge whether or not it is just and good for their people. They don't need the consensus to rule. Now I'm not suggesting public officials should start governing without legislative authority, but clearly we can learn something valuable from Lincoln's example: when a public servant is committed to a respected higher authority than the written body of laws, the laws themselves are improved and given new life.

Lincoln's faith in a metaphysical world of values was closely linked to his belief that a divine hand was at work in American history. Eventually, he came to see the war as a manifestation of divine intervention: "I am almost ready to say . . . that God wills this contest, and wills that it shall not end yet." Lincoln believed that God could "have either saved or destroyed the Union without a human contest," and "having begun He could give the final victory to either side any day. Yet the contest proceeds. In the present civil war, it is quite possible that God's purpose is something different from the purpose of either party." Perhaps God "permits the war for some wise purpose of his own, mysterious and unknown to us."[93]

The President possessed a strong sense of duty to an all-knowing and just deity to whom he would have to answer. Two

---

92. Donald, *Lincoln*, p. 442
93. Donald, *Lincoln*, p. 371

examples can serve to illustrate his awareness of his responsibility in this regard. Shortly after Gettysburg, following a meeting with a group of Christians from Chicago who were encouraging emancipation, Lincoln told his cabinet he had made a vow, a covenant, that if God gave the Union victory in the approaching battle, he would consider it an indication of divine will that he should move forward in the cause of emancipation.[94] Lincoln was true to his word. Following the pardon of a number of Indians condemned to death for the Indian uprising in Minnesota in the fall of 1863, Senator Ramsey admonished Lincoln for the pardons, telling him that if he had hanged more Indians he would have had a larger majority in the coming election. Lincoln responded simply, "I could not afford to hang men for votes."[95]

If only our politicians today could restrain themselves from buying their offices at the price of children's lives! How many have changed their once pro-life position to appease a demanding electorate? Once upon a time William Clinton, Al Gore, and Mayor Daley of Chicago, to name a few, were pro-life. They sold out to win campaigns. And win them they did. But little evils lead to greater evils. The guilt of one murder turned Shakespeare's Macbeth into a hardened killer covered with the blood of hundreds by the end of the play. Does Bill Clinton realize that he has traveled the same road? How else can we understand his refusal to prohibit partial birth abortion? When even the American Medical Association has told him that such a procedure is never necessary to save the life of the mother, what could possibly have moved him to such action?

The Development of Doctrine and the Constitution

Speaking again from my Catholic formation, I find in the history of Constitutional interpretation something that bears a

---

94. Donald, *Lincoln*, p. 374
95. Donald, *Lincoln*, p. 385

remarkable similarity to what we call the "Development of Doctrine" in the Church. Constitutional amendments parallel in a certain way dogma's defined by the Church that are not literally to be found in the Bible. Teachings such as that of the Immaculate Conception grow from a deeper understanding of Biblical texts. Something similar happened in American Constitutional law following the Emancipation Proclamation. Without specifically being stated in the Constitution, the equal dignity of African-Americans could be assumed from the fundamental truths that the Founding Fathers had written into that document and the Declaration of Independence. I would go so far as to say that this insight saved this nation after the Civil War by releasing the real though hidden potential of the Constitution.

Most students of Constitutional law are familiar with the distinction between "strict constructionists" and "loose constructionists." These represent the two classic approaches to interpretation of the Constitution and most judges on the Supreme Court will fall into one of these categories. The strict constructionists stand by the law as it is actually written. They understand the role of judge to be strictly guardian and interpreter of the Constitution just as it reads. They cherish the concrete application of the law and eschew abstract theorizing. If the Constitution needs changing, they maintain, it includes the processes necessary to do so. In fact, the Constitution has been altered twenty-seven times already, about every seven years. But judges do not and cannot change the law — they only apply what has been decided by elected representatives of the people.

Loose constructionists, on the other hand, believe that the Constitution is a living, flexible document and the responsibility of judges is to make a bridge between the high ideals of the framers of the Constitution and the actual needs of our time. Loose constructionists stand for a freedom in interpretation that will allow issues to be resolved quickly without awaiting the cumbersome and time-consuming process of constitutional amendment. The essential aspect of the Constitution which judges are bound to apply with ever increasing zeal is the protection of individual civil liberties.

But the discussion cannot end here. Whether a judge espouses strict constructionism or loose constructionism is still not enough. In regards to slavery, the strict constructionists used their philosophical position to defend the property rights of the South. They reasoned that since the framers of the Constitution did not intend civil liberties to extend to African-Americans, they themselves had no power to change the laws. They could only apply what they read in the law. The result: a defense of Southern property rights. Furthermore, the loose constructionists put themselves forward as defenders of freedom — with the restriction that the freedom in question was that of the white man, not the black.

How amazing the parallel to the abortion debate! Because the Constitution says nothing about abortion, strict constructionists will strike down any law prohibiting abortion because "it's not in the Constitution." And, on the other side of the coin, the loose constructionists will strike down the same laws in the name of the mother's right to privacy. Both, feeling quite content with themselves, believe they have been faithful to the Constitution.

The problem is that methods of interpretation cannot exist separate from fundamental truths. Truth is the light that must shine on systems and applications, otherwise we are a nation of computers not human beings. The development of doctrine that I mentioned in the history of the Catholic faith — so beautifully described by Cardinal Newman — was possible because of the immutable nature of truth. The difficulty for the theologian — or in our present discussion, the judge — is to distinguish between the unchanging truths and the particular practices that are meant to embody these truths.

Consider the way Lincoln and countless others developed from a moderate position against slavery, the so-called "anti-expansionist" position, to full-fledged abolitionism. What is to be noted is that within this perspective of "anti-expansionism" lay the seed of the immutable truth that lies at the heart of the abolitionist's position. Lincoln's starting point was based on two praiseworthy beliefs ultimately shown to be incompatible. He felt strong disdain for the idea of humans owning other humans; but he also felt great sympathy for the Southern farm owners and the grand lifestyle that the South had worked so hard to establish. In both cases Lincoln wanted to cherish the principle of human liberty — but this truth translated into practice meant that slavery had to go.

In the development of doctrine an essential tenet is that truth can never contradict itself. Slavery was based on a fundamental error and no matter how firmly it might have been entrenched in practice, it could not ultimately co-exist with the high ideals of the Constitution. At first, Lincoln's acceptance of slavery was like a storeowner who tolerates kids steeling candy from his candy barrel. He knows it's wrong, but what are you going to do about it? To take action against his little thieves, the storeowner doesn't have to make a 180° about-face in his moral position; rather, he must put a limit to his tolerance. He already has a clear understanding of what is right and wrong. Today, most moderates believe that abortion is wrong, but certainly not bad enough to be the object of intolerance. That is because abortion does not have the ugly face of say the Ku Klux Klan or the Nazi death camps.

A situation I faced in my diocese regarding this point is worth mentioning to illustrate the need for a more honest approach on the part of "moderates."

During my first years as a priest, the diocesan marriage preparation office recruited me to give talks at the mandatory Pre-Cana conferences. It was an excellent opportunity to strengthen the faith of the many couples who attended and introduce them to the Church's marvelous teachings on marriage. When the subject of birth control and contraception came up, I showed a slide presentation on Natural Family Planning from the Couple to Couple League. It was a basic discussion of the issue, very positive and pastoral, but clearly committed to Catholic moral principles about the sanctity of marriage, sexuality, and human life. At a certain point in the presentation the narrator suggested a link between the failure of contraception and the escalation of abortion. These words were accompanied by a picture of abortive remains. That one picture was sited by several participants who had been educated in Catholic schools and knew enough about Catholic hierarchy to have me "fired" from the program. Clearly, they did not accept the Church's teaching on contraception. But the greater responsibility lay with the Church authorities who missed this valuable opportunity to represent the Church's teaching in truth and encourage these members of the flock to reflect on these fundamental issues. Regretably the director "fired me" from giving further talks. Such office holders at the heart of the Church are comparable to men such as Seward, Vallandigham, or McClellan who held positions that would have allowed them to destroy slavery, but chose instead the moderate position, claiming to oppose slavery personally while at the same time dismantling the efforts of abolitionists.

Usually, a development in doctrine comes about as a defense against heresy. An encounter with evil can serve to clarify the good, rather like a vaccination that builds up the body's natural defenses by inserting a tiny piece of a disease. Lincoln's understanding of the Constitution developed radically as a result of his experience of slave trading only a few blocks from the White House. Even though he maintained that the business of society was still thriving, the business of that poor black fellow's life was not. Sooner or later, and I pray it is sooner, Americans will be jolted into a similar realization about abortion: that those who have had abortions have really hurt another human being — beyond repair — and are themselves damaged for life. That is why, as ugly as they are, it is important to display pictures of aborted fetuses in public since doing so is one of the few ways of helping people see what is really going on. They act on the conscience just like the open whippings at slave markets helped develop the conscience of our sixteenth President.

The bitter and lengthy experience of civil war tested the moderate anti-expansionist position and demanded a development of constitutional doctrine. It pushed society to look slavery squarely in the face, not simply as a means to some other end. Slavery had to be judged either as a good in itself, and worthy of preservation, or an intrinsic evil against which all the powers of the nation had to be directed. The inconsistency of saying "Owning slaves is good for some people, but I don't think I would ever own a slave" or "The South should be able to retain slavery, but I don't think new settlers in the West should own slaves" became more and more evident. If slavery is a good, how can one limit it at all? If it is an evil, how can one defend it? That's the same story with abortion. There's no way around deciding this question. Either abortion is a good or it is an evil. The answer to this question should determine our government's policy on abortion just as it did on slavery. How long can we keep up the charade of saying, "I'm personally opposed to abortion but I think it should be legal and safe for women who want one."

Social injustice that is ignored for too long eventually corrodes the heart of a people. Putting an end to slavery was not just good for the slaves, it was good for the whole country. One could say that the nation was restored to health by the Emancipation Proclamation. Moderates should meditate on this fact and realize the menace of their position. They look at our society like the store owner views the operation of his store, willing to accept a little shoplifting since overall he's doing good business. However, as any good mother or father knows, one disciplines a child for stealing, not so much out of a concern for the successful operation of a business, but because of the negative effect stealing will have on a child's character and personality. It's not good for the child to steal, even before one considers the effects of the practice on society at large. Moderates tolerate liberal abortion laws because it seems that the "business of society" is not too seriously damaged by abortion, without any regard to the daily, personal agony inflicted on the unborn and the lifelong, debilitating regret hoisted on the mother — not to mention the depersonalizing effect of abortion on the medical personnel involved. Abortion destroys human beings in more ways than one.

Pardon and Peace

Americans are famous the world over for their informal approach and ready to wear friendship. One aspect of American conviviality is our readiness to forgive. We like to forgive — maybe because forgiveness is forward moving and Americans are a practical people. Why cry over spilt milk? Why wallow in regret? Let's rebuild! In all her military conflicts, American victory has always been followed by a period of magnanimous reconstruction of the former enemy's land and goods. The situation was no less so following our own civil war. That is not to say that the bitterness of defeat and sorrow over a "lost cause" did not continue to linger in the hearts of many Southerners. One can find traces of it to this day. But whatever personal feelings may have existed, the population as a whole recognized the need to forgive and move onward in the new direction that the war had opened up for the nation.

Perhaps this aspect of the story leaps out at me so much because of my role as Catholic priest. My job takes me into the confessional where I receive the repentance of sinners and offer them the consoling words of God's forgiveness which we call "absolution." I have witnessed the peace that follows a good confession and I know the power of repentance and forgiveness for the reconstruction of the individual and the society in which he lives.

The first step on the road to reconciliation is to recognize one's fault and ask forgiveness. If this is at times difficult for the individual it is even more rare to find world leaders asking for the forgiveness on behalf of their people. I can only think of one such leader in our own time who has had the courage to do so: Pope John Paul II. Throughout his pontificate he has issued statements of apology and regret to many who have in any way suffered from the misuse and abuse of Church power through the ages. He officially cleared Galileo from the condemnation he received at the Church's hands. He has made highly visible appearances with the representatives of other faiths and publicly asked for their pardon. The climax of his efforts at reconciliation was reached at the beginning of Lent in this Jubilee Year. First, The International Theological Commission published a document entitled, "*Memory and Reconciliation: The Church and the Faults of the Past,*" in which the Church asked pardon for crimes such as the atrocities committed during the crusades, anti-Semitism, and the oppression of women. Then, John Paul II declared Sunday, March 12, 2000 a "Day of Pardon." In his homily that day he remarked:

> **Let us forgive and ask forgiveness!** *While we praise God who, in his merciful love, has produced in the Church a wonderful harvest of holiness, missionary zeal, total dedication to Christ and neighbor, we cannot fail to recognize* **the infidelities to the Gospel committed by some of our brethren,** *especially during the second millennium. Let us ask pardon for the divisions which have occurred among Christians, for the violence some have used in the service of truth and for the distrustful and hostile attitudes sometimes taken towards the followers of other religions.*
>
> *Let us confess, even more,* **our responsibility as Christians for the evils of today.** *We must ask ourselves what our responsibilities are regarding atheism, religious indifference, secularism, ethical relativism, the violations of the right to life, disregard for the poor in many countries.*
>
> *We humbly ask forgiveness for the part which each of us has had in these evils by our own actions, thus helping to disfigure the face of the Church.*

Perhaps there are members of other religious denominations, scientific bodies, or ethnic groups who feel regret for their crimes against humanity, or the Catholic Church in particular, but none of them to my knowledge has asked for pardon. If I am wrong, I would like to be corrected. In most cases, such an apology is not even possible since no "visible head" can speak for these groups of people. Most people see the papacy's only job as proclaiming doctrines of faith and morals, but clearly the present Holy Father understands the Chair of St. Peter as a vehicle for humbling acts of virtue — a light shining in an age of despair!

My purpose in highlighting these efforts of the Holy Father is to demonstrate the power and necessity of pardon in the reconstruction of society. A policy of pardon made all the difference in the years following the Civil War. Abraham Lincoln made it absolutely clear that pardon was to be extended to all those who sought it. His only aim was full restoration of the Union. In general, the men who succeeded Lincoln followed this plan. Pardon was asked for and granted, with some notable exceptions. It is these exceptions which draw us deeper into an understanding of what is strongest in our national character. At the same time, we can catch the back draft of what most threatens us.

The federal government has pardoned both Jefferson Davis and Robert E. Lee. Most people probably do not realize that these two champions of the Confederacy may now hold public office. I bet, though, that if you asked the ordinary American who is held in higher esteem, Lee or Davis, the answer would most likely be Lee. If we take a closer look at this popular sentiment, we can discern something about the nature of pardon that may help us in the future.

What I am referring to is the fact that Lee's post-war attitude was quite different from that of Davis. Lee in fact was a much better model of the repentant American. Despite the fact that he had waged war on the United States for five years — with remarkable success — following the Civil War he dedicated himself to reconciliation. In August of 1865 he wrote in a letter, "The questions which were in dispute having been decided against us, it is the part of wisdom to acquiesce in the result, and of candor to recognize the fact. The interests of the State are therefore the same as those of the United States. Its prosperity will rise or fall with the welfare of the country. The duty of its citizens, then, appears to me too plain to admit of doubt. All should unite in honest efforts to obliterate the effects of war, and to restore the blessings of peace."

Lee asked for official pardon in June of 1865. Whether it was the result of Southern pride, or just a clerical oversight, he didn't send the required oath of loyalty until September. Officials in the War Department misplaced it and it remained undiscovered in the National Archives until 1970. Finally, in August of 1975, President Gerald Ford signed Senate Joint Resolution 23 restoring full citizenship rights to Robert E. Lee.

Yet Robert E. Lee's incredible gallantry was not appreciated by all. His appointment to the presidency of Washington College in Lexington, Virginia was seen by some in the North as a travesty of justice. One journalist pronounced him unfit to train the youth of Virginia. In the North he was for a long time associated with Benedict Arnold. Nonetheless, Lee's worth as a leader was proven not only on the field of battle, but in the even more difficult challenges of the reconstruction years. He showed himself able to humble himself so that the state he loved could be lifted up and walk with confidence into a happier and more prosperous future.

This was not to be the case with Jefferson Davis. The President of the Confederate States of America received his own pardon in November of 1978 when President Jimmy Carter approved congressional action extending amnesty to Jefferson Davis. Yet, when one compares the lives of Davis and Lee after the South's surrender, it is difficult to understand Carter's action. In fact, the bestowal of this pardon reveals more about the contemporary American moral dilemma than it does about the character of Jefferson Davis. The fact is Davis went to his dying days unconvinced of the errors of his ways. Late in life, he proclaimed, "It's been said that I should apply to the United States for a pardon. But repentance must precede the right of pardon and I have not repented! Remembering as I must all which has been lost, disappointed hopes and crushed aspirations, yet I deliberately say, if it were to do over again I would do just as I did in 1861."[96]

This attitude is evidence that Davis pushed the war effort from much more deeply held philosophical motivations than did Lee. Perhaps he was more astute at realizing the connection between the South's prosperity and slavery than Lee was. Lee must not have thought about slavery much, and he is even on record as opposing it. He is more worthy of American esteem because, as is clear from his own words, he fought not to retain slavery but simply for his homeland, his beloved Virginia.

In my role as Catholic priest I have to apply the Church's understanding of the kinds and degrees of sin. There are some that are very serious which we call *mortal sins*; and others that are not so serious that we call *venial* sins. It's an important distinction that allows a confessor to judge the actions of a soul and guide him or her to peaceful reconciliation with God. When we consider the choices made by those who fought for the South during the Civil War, I believe some such distinction must be made. The fact that America has bestowed on Robert E. Lee a degree of hero status shows that Americans do, in fact, though unconsciously perhaps, apply this distinction. In one sense, Lee's "sins" may have been greater than the "sins" of Davis. After all, he was more personally responsible for individual deaths on the battlefield. But Lee's ignorance of the full meaning of his actions mitigates his guilt. Further, his humility and repentance clearly make possible restoration of the unity that had been lost.

What makes Jefferson Davis's pardon so difficult is that he did not want to be pardoned. Doesn't it seem strange that we would

---

96. Francis MacDonnell, *Reconstruction in the Wake of Vietnam, The Pardoning of Lee and Davis*, Civil War History, vol. 1 (Kent State, OH: Kent State University Press, March 1995, p. 122

cover a man with forgiveness when he clearly does not want the reconciliation offered?

The premise of this book is that the real cause of the Civil War has all but disappeared from our telling of the story. The pardon of Jefferson Davis serves as an example of this cultural shift. In order to pardon Davis, it is necessary to believe that all opinions are equal and no judgement can ever possibly be made of a man's choices. If this is true, where is the pardon for Mussolini, Hitler, and Stalin? Too radical a question? If you think so, have you forgotten that Jefferson Davis served as president over a regime dedicated to the enslavement of human beings? Does that make it more clear? Furthermore, he did not acknowledge the error of his convictions. According to his own words, he would have placed all his efforts once again behind the attempt to re-establish that regime. Yet, this is the man that our Congress and our President covered with forgiveness.

This reflection on the nature of pardon and its role in the years following the Civil War serves to illuminate the situation in which we now find ourselves as legalized abortion faces inevitable extinction. In the last few years, we have seen remarkable conversions from the pro-abortion side of the argument to staunch pro-life activism. The most famous of these are no doubt the very women whose names are associated with the 1973 Supreme Court decision: Norma McCorvey — the Jane Roe of *Roe v. Wade*, and Sandra Cano — the Jane Doe of *Doe v. Bolton*. Another outstanding example of repentance and conversion is Dr. Bernard Nathanson, one time guiding hand of the National Abortion Rights Action League. Thanks to Dr. Nathanson's raw personal honesty, we have an insight into the motivations and tactics of the death mongers who are preying on our nation's women and children. It is important to consider these highly visible and public conversions because we can find in them the patience and hope necessary to lead our nation back into the light. Human beings are not fated to evil; they are capable of conversion. Let us be ready, as Americans always have been, to cover our repentant brothers and sisters with pardon and peace.

Temper Tantrums (or How the South Won the War)

At the end of every military conflict there are, among the defeated, those who accept the reality of defeat and acquiesce to the demands of the victors, and those who will not acknowledge the facts, choosing instead to remain unchanged in opinion or action, cloaking themselves in the glory of a "lost cause." If the cause were a noble one to begin with, such fidelity is admirable. If, however, justice has truly triumphed in the conflict, those who persist in their error are like an abscess leaking slow poison into society's veins.

Such was the post-war obstinacy of Alexander Stephens, vice president of the Confederate States of America. It had been Stephens's famous "cornerstone speech" which expressed in the purest terms the real cause of the Civil War and the crux of the South's argument with the North:

> *It is the Republican threat to slavery which is the immediate cause of the late rupture and the present revolution of Confederate independence. The old confederation known as the United States had been founded on the false idea that all men are created equal. The new Confederacy, by contrast is founded upon exactly the opposite idea: its foundations are laid, its cornerstone rests upon the great truth that the Negro is not equal to the white man, that slavery, subordination to the superior race, is his natural and normal condition. This, our new government, is the first in the history of the world, based on this great physical, philosophical, and moral truth.*[97]

---

97. McPherson, *What They Fought For, 1861-1865*, p. 48

After the war, Stephens, like many Southern intellectuals, wrote about the event, striving to explain and justify the Confederate rebellion. In his post-war book — and note the title — A Constitutional View of the Late War Between the States, Stephens stated his constitutional theory:

> *Some of the strongest anti-slavery men who ever lived were on the side of those who opposed the North and their Centralization principle which lead to the war. The war was a strife between the principles of Federation on the one side, and Centralism, or Consolidation on the other . . . The Federationists [the Southerners] opposed the Emancipation Proclamation because they saw it as a first step in many future measures. Their opposition to that measure, or kindred subsequent ones, spring from no attachment to slavery; but as Jefferson's, Pinkney's and Clay's, from their strong convictions that the Federal Government has no rightful or Constitutional control or jurisdiction over such questions, and that no such action as that proposed upon them could be taken by Congress without destroying the elementary and vital principles upon which the government was founded . . . It was not a contest between the advocates or opponents of that peculiar institution, but a contest between the supporters of a strictly Federative Government on the one side, and a thoroughly National one on the other.*[98]

Stephens sets forth in the most articulate, juridical language a "noble rationalization" which brilliantly diverts attention away from the otherwise guilt-producing topic of slavery. The Northern

---

98. Alexander Stephens, *A Constitutional View of the late War Between the States* (Chicago/St. Louis: National Publishing Co., Zeigler, McCurdy & Co., 1886), p. 11

victory had made it impossible for him to re-give his 1862 speech; thus, as is so often the case when one finds oneself the loser of a conflict, he comes up with a different defense instead of a hearty apology. I ask, how much good could have been done if he, as a leading spokesman of the Confederacy, had repented of their crimes against the black race? What future pain and turmoil between blacks and whites might have been eased if words of sorrow and regret were offered in place of an unceasing self-righteousness?

Casualty of War

Taking another look at Alexander Stephens's post-war philosophizing, it is very important to see the purely utilitarian references he makes regarding Jefferson, Pinkney and Clay. He refers again and again to these men throughout his book, not because they thought so much like him, but because they provided an extremely rare example of Southern abolitionists who fought for the Southern Cause. Stephens needs these examples if he is to succeed in his claim that the Civil War was not about slavery but about the infringement of nationalism. To the jury of America he points to these three Confederate heroes as proof that the South was not really fighting to keep slavery. His efforts in this regard display one of histories shrewdest sales jobs, and most of America bought it.

But if we can manage to disentangle ourselves from his rhetoric for a moment, we will take note that Stephens's obstinate refusal to re-examine his own opinions resulted in a casualty of war sadder than any other, yet less recognized than the bones of the unknown soldier. Stephens and his confreres placed a wedge between the theoretical world of political rhetoric and the practical world of everyday life. The immediate fallout of this separation is the notion, "You are automatically wrong if you are telling me what to do." With truth so disabled, a slow, metastasizing cancer entered the American conscience and sank its roots deep into the national psyche. We are so accustomed to the presence of this lie that we take it for granted as a first principle in our decisions. As a result, one could say that the South really won the Civil War. She has risen again gloriously triumphant as she always said she would.

Imagine if you will our nation as a family, with the North, the victors playing the role of mother and the South being the scolded son. The scolded son Johnny is told that he can't go out and play until he cleans his room. Johnny, of course, doesn't want to clean his room and very much wants to go out and play. Johnny assures mom that he most certainly will clean his room later, right after he is finished playing. Mom recalls the past five times Johnny has made such a promise and his failure to follow through. She takes her stand on her first order. Johnny screams and yells and runs around. But his mother prevails and the room is cleaned. While Johnny is so occupied, his friends have come and gone. He is now doubly furious and holds his mom as incompetent. He believes his anger is justified. Hasn't he suffered at the hands of an arbitrary, unfeeling power? Did he not promise compliance, but in his own time and in his own way?

Let us analyze the logic of the screaming child. What would be Johnny's defense? "Mom, why did you make me clean my room? I would have done it when I got back." Mom, meanwhile, is thinking, "I wasn't born yesterday."

In little Johnny's attitude there is a fear or hatred of being told what to do. We can kind of excuse Johnny because it is natural for little boys to prefer playing outside to cleaning their rooms. However, this inner resentment of following directions from legitimate superiors often has no other basis than the realization that the action required is not one's own idea. In other words, I'm not the origin of the order, so I hate the order and the one who makes it. The person feels his or her freedom has been taken away, simply because they are subject to the directions of another. Such an attitude can and does reek great havoc in many community settings. The typical rebuttal of one forced to do something against one's will is, "I was going to do it anyway." Unfortunately, too many people realize the weakness of these words when it comes to children promising to clean their rooms, but fail to see the same weakness when it comes to larger, more weighty decisions in the public sphere concerning the rights of others.

Such fits of anger are not limited to children. I had personal experience of this kind of behavior in my own home diocese. In the early 1990's our Bishop had to close down a number of parishes. In his judgement these were not "cost effective." He knew it would not be a popular decision, and tried to let the people down slowly. He conducted many "listening sessions" on the matter. From his perspective, these listening sessions were primarily supposed to help the people understand his dilemma and build respect for his decision to close the parishes. Secondarily, they may have brought to light some facts or details that might have altered his decision. The people who attended the sessions, on the other hand, supposed the sessions were their chance to prove to the bishop that it was wrong to close the parishes. Now, one can say that there is certainly something very admirable about people who "fight downtown" to keep their churches open — would that everyone in the neighborhood had felt the say way and fought the same fight! But alas, many did not. In fact, that was at the heart of the problem all the time. If there were hundreds more who would have worked to keep these churches open, the bishop would never have been in the position of having to close them.

After the closings were effected, a mysterious Stephens-esque attitude was expressed by those who had fought to keep the churches open: "Well, we realized they had to be closed eventually, and the bishop had to do what he had to do, but . . . we object to the way he did it." Can you see the similarity of logic? What they were in effect saying was, "Our anger is not based on whether or not the churches stay open, but on the fact that the bishop just marched in and told us what we had to do." Those who express this opinion would have us believe that they themselves would have closed the churches in due time if they had been given the opportunity. Alexander Stephens wanted us to believe the same thing about the South and slavery. In essence, he was saying, "We Southerners were not angry because you Northerners were telling us to do away with slavery; we were mad because you were ordering us to do something." But Stephens's argument can't stand. In order for it to be true, the South would have had to be ambivalent about slavery and have every intention of doing away with it on their own had not the North forced the event upon them. We know that this was not the case.

This kind of intellectual stubbornness follows the refusal to admit error in thought or action. It is, in short, pride. In the world of philosophy, intellectual positions can be held like fortresses in the mind. Opinions can be defended from all attacks. Even when all the reasons in the world have shown the error of an opinion, the will of the person can still hold the fort by the sheer refusal to accept the truth. It's a "to the death" confrontation because truth means a change in behavior. Injustice often hides behind firmly held, unexamined opinions. In the Civil War, the theoretical language of rights was absolutely grounded in the practice of holding slaves. The desire to continue this practice fed the fire of intellectual speculation and produced serpentine arguments easily adaptable to changing circumstances. Yesterday it was slavery, today slavery has nothing to do with it, and tomorrow it will be something else. We have seen the same mental gymnastics in the pro-abortion line of argument, running the gamut from the horror of back street abortions, to saving the poor from unwanted pregnancies, to a woman's right over her own body, etc. And underneath all the inventions of the mind is the daily practice of murdering the innocent.

Actually, the pro-life position has never been so poised to tear down legalized abortion. So many of the popular arguments in favor of abortion have proved to be so blatantly false that we can at least speak now in plain language. Isn't abortion really about "not telling me what to do"? Wouldn't the argument run something like this: "I don't want to have this baby, and that's all you need to know to allow me an abortion. I don't need to give you reasons. The only one that matters is that I don't want to be pregnant."

Legalized abortion, then, represents the legal entrenchment of Alexander Stephens's position. Truth or error, justice or injustice has no place anymore in American law. The only thing that matters is that Johnny can do what he wants. Our American liberties have been reduced to the volatile whims of a spoiled child.

Pro-lifers can learn a lot from the post-war brooding of some Confederate leaders. Not only can they give us a clue to the vehemence behind the pro-abortion position, but they also show us what we can expect to hear when the Roe v. Wade decision is reversed or a human life amendment has been added to our Constitution. Many will say, "We are angry now, not so much because we support the right to abortion, but we are angry at the fact that some people in Washington are telling us what we can or can't do." In the end, the argument always winds up the same: "You're the bad guy, not because I didn't want to do what you were asking me to do, but because you were forcing me to do it."

What is to be done with the disobedient child? Hopefully, time and maturity will help him realize that his own will is not threatened by the truthful voice of another; and the freedom he cherishes is made complete by his participation in the common good. He will hopefully acquire the humility of heart to place his own interests at the service of justice. If not, he will be a criminal, and society will eventually have to deal with him in ways that will deprive him of his freedom. We must look very carefully at Alexander Stephens's principle because a society immersed in it can never build a vital respect for proper or lawful authority. We will remain a society of children who don't really know what they want, except that they don't want to be told what to do.

The Whole Person

The individual is of paramount importance in American life. The high value we place on each individual life separates us dramatically at times from other cultures. During World War II, for example, the Japanese were astounded and bewildered by the American concern for the survival of the wounded. They could not, for instance, believe that the American Navy would decorate a man for saving two damaged American warships and guiding them to home base with their crews, "Americans thrill to all rescue, all aid to those pressed to the wall. A valiant deed is all the more a hero's act if is saves the 'damaged.' "[99]

Even our heroes and our popular stories hold out to us in various guises the glory of the individual. Gary Cooper in *High Noon* is an archetype of the lonesome cowboy who triumphs over a host of enemies. We love the underdog and cherish stories of the guy from nowhere with nothing who reaches the highest office in the land: Abraham Lincoln, for example. The fact that such a thing can happen proves again and again that America is the land of freedom and opportunity of which our forefathers dreamed. American law, we believe, exists to guarantee and protect each individual's right to freely choose his or her destiny.

American individualism is arguably two sides of the same coin: on the one hand, love and respect for the value of a single human life, and on the other, an egoism that leads to a flagrant disregard for the good of others. Yet, in the name of the good of that single individual, Americans will allow all kinds of action that may or may not be good for society. Better to risk an abuse than to lose the smallest portion of our freedom.

The deep respect of Americans for the right of the individual to realize his destiny was one of the saving graces that carried this

---

99. Ruth Benedict, *The Chrysanthemum and the Sword: Patterns of Japanese Culture* (New York, NY: New American Library, Inc., 1974), p. 36

country forward after the Civil War. We learned that race is not a sufficient reason for denying an individual's rights. Although injustice against men of color continued, and though the South was well trodden under the heels of the carpetbaggers for years, the Constitution itself had been opened up to the future in such a way that within a hundred years the labor pains of the new birth of freedom would deliver a nation of equals before the law irrespective of race or gender. (The woman's suffrage movement was an immediate spin-off of the efforts of abolitionists.)

The challenge today is to take that appreciation of the human person a step further — to the personhood of the unborn child. If America could only see the truth of the pro-life ideology, she would recognize and embrace it with open arms as her own heart and soul. It's simply this: where there is a human being there is a person; where there is a person, there is the right to the fundamental liberties of "life, liberty, and the pursuit of happiness." This IS the soul of America. When we speak of the Right to Life movement, we mean nothing else than an expansion of the rights guaranteed in the Constitution to ALL human beings, *in utero* or *ex utero* (in the womb or out of the womb). We are calling for the same kind of quantum leap forward that it took our nation to see in the black man a person and a citizen equally protected by the Constitution. Pro-lifers want to push the ceiling on the Constitution.

The good to be derived from pro-life goals far exceeds protecting the life of the unborn. The pro-life point of view opens an avenue for the resolution of all kinds of social problems because it provides a first principle, a foundation upon which to start. To affirm the value and dignity of each individual human life is to take the person as a whole — body and soul, intellect, will and desires — everything that makes a person a person. Whatever good we do for others, however we approach the problems of hunger, disease, and over-population, or the moral sufferings of loneliness, depression, and addictions, we do so with this vision of the integral value of the whole person. Pro-life philosophy assumes that life is a good and killing innocent people is never a solution, neither for the suffering individual nor the society in which he lives.

We have already discussed the separation of heart and head implied by a pro-abortion mindset. Anti-life means piecemeal thinking about the individual, seeing him or her as a conglomeration of parts that we can separate at will. Solutions to society's problems at present reflect this overly simplistic view of the human being that addresses only isolated aspects of the person. A good example is the two classic approaches to sex education. There are those who target merely the intellectual side of the person: "If we just tell our young people a lot about sex early on . . . if we replace ignorance with knowledge . . ." On the other hand, some people would rather leap over the intellectual factor and address the merely physical aspects of the person: "Don't expect young people to think. Hand out condoms instead. Make sure abortion is readily available to teenagers." Both approaches have been dismal failures.

When we consider efforts to resolve the problem of poverty in our society we see these two philosophies at work again. The first group advocates incessantly the need for education. Children must be educated more on the reality of poverty, farmers must be educated to advance agricultural science, couples must be educated on methods of birth control, including abortion, to reduce population, etc. On the other side of the coin, the physical aspects of the person are the sole aim. The solution to poverty is filling stomachs. What we need are more bread lines and soup kitchens and homeless shelters. The government should pass out more food stamps.

If we remain limited to either of these two approaches it seems that we are doomed to be forever frustrated in our attempts to eliminate social problems. This is not because these approaches are wrong in themselves; it is, rather, that they are incomplete.

Neither approach of itself can solve the problem of world hunger. The enlightenment of the mind naively assumes that smart people are automatically generous people. Unfortunately, just the opposite is often the case. Some of the greediest people in the world are very well educated. On the other hand, the free distribution of goods may feed people for a day or a week or a year, but such ongoing assistance tends to destroy their own initiative to provide for themselves and keep them from growing towards self-sufficiency. It also assumes that there will always be givers with a surplus to spare, that is not always the case, as we know.

What America is realizing as we enter this new millennium, even though our major political trends generally gravitate to one or the other, is that neither of these views works. Work with the poor and teach them how to fish, or raise taxes so we can buy them more fish that other people catch — it still comes out to the same in the end. At best, there are those who would propose a balance between the two; but this tactic still falls short of real human potential. What we need to do is get away from simplistic reductions of the human person. True enough, the body and the intellect are two vital aspects of the person, but the person is not defined solely in terms of these two. The human person is a complicated creature indeed. There is, for instance, the will, the desires, and the passions, as well as the full social context in which the person lives: his history, culture and traditions, not to mention his creed or philosophy of life.

The will is perhaps the least considered by the two approaches I have described above. A pessimistic age has left us with a very low opinion of human nature: you can't expect people to do the right thing, so systems have to be put in place to push and prod good behavior out of them. In a sense, the individual is a pawn to be moved about by someone else, certainly not by his own initiative. Yet, human dignity rests in the capacity to acknowledge the good and move towards it. Proposed solutions to social problems will always be seriously handicapped unless the will is taken seriously and respected. Placing the individual in the driver's seat of his or her own life reintegrates the person and brings into play all aspects of his or her unique history and personality.

The Contraceptive Mentality

At this juncture we have to ask a difficult question: How have we happened on such a piecemeal approach to the human person? What has shattered the wholeness of the individual person which lies at the heart of the American Dream?

Once again, we can glean insight from the past. Just as slavery rose from the seedbed of an immature philosophy of the human person, abortion appeared as the fruit of a society that had steadily acquiesced to grievous errors about the human being and the nature of human happiness. Until we as a people can face up to these errors, no amount of effort against legalized abortion will ultimately succeed. We must go deeper.

At the beginning of this century, family planning was hailed as a forward moving step for society. True, responsible parenthood is to be advocated. But hand in hand with the idea of the planned family came the use of a new technology that allowed a couple to practice artificial contraception: the Pill. In the initial exuberance of this event no careful reflection was made as to the long term effects of artificial contraception. Only later did doctors begin to discover that a woman's hormonal system was a delicate balance deserving the outmost respect. You can't use a woman's body as a test tube. But even beyond the medical problems of the Pill, the impact of contraceptive practice on the person, on marriage, on society as a whole, has finally begun to receive more attention. We are getting "to the roots" of the matter and instead of basing our decisions on a simplistic reduction of the human being to a mere collection of cells, we are understanding the less obvious but more important dimensions of human nature.

The error of contraception is one of the subtlest errors of the modern world. At this point, I can hear the clamor, "What would you expect a priest to say?" But contraception is not wrong because the Church says so; the Church condemns contraception because it is wrong. The Andrew Grealey's of the church notwithstanding. In this regard, the Catholic Church has been way ahead of its time.

When everyone wanted to say that sex was just about the body, the Church held and still holds that human sexuality is connected to love and to that uniquely human possibility of self-donation which leads to a happy life and a healthy society. The Church upholds a "holistic" view of the person. Although we can split the ideas "body" and "soul" in our minds, they are in reality intimately bound and inseparable. You can't play around with one without affecting the other.

Those who practice contraception introduce into their marriage a slow poison that corrupts from the inside. A subtle shift of view and feeling takes place over the years until the moral conscience is no longer disturbed by manipulations of the body. Though a contracepting person may not express this in so many words, the mentality is such that he/she is in essence saying, "Though I am doing this to my body or your body, I am not doing it to you as a person." A divide is introduced between "the person" and "the person's body." They are no longer one thing, but two. Therefore, you can get away with anything you do to the body because, so you think, you are not adversely effecting the person.

Perhaps a further analogy might help illustrate this point.

Imagine there is a man who desperately wants to play baseball. He dreams of it day and night. To know the person John Smith is to know a person who wants to shine on the baseball field. Now, suppose John had a girlfriend named Jane who loved everything about John, but just couldn't stand his aspirations to become a baseball champion. The relationship could still be basically a good one, despite the fact that Jane does not particularly like John's deep professional inclinations. What if, however, Jane is not content to simply grumble inwardly to herself about John's desires but instead takes an active roll in defeating his efforts to realize them? Say, for instance, she gets a call from a professional scout while John is out of town and tells the scout, "Sorry, John isn't interested in your offer." What do you think John's reaction will be when he gets home? If you guessed "upset, fuming mad, near volcanic," you'd be right.

What is the moral to this story? How does it relate to the contraceptive issue? The moral is that the fullness of John's personhood includes his incredible desire to be a baseball player. In John's opinion, if someone is to truly love him as a whole person, his baseball-ness must be included. "Love me, love my dog," as the French say.

In the matter of contraceptive sexual behavior, baby-free sexual joys are the goal while dominance over the body's natural tendency toward fertility is the means. The body, then, is relegated to the role of "instrument" to achieve the heart's desire. Mind over matter in a pure sense. Like the inconsiderate girlfriend who tries to sabotage her boyfriend's ambitions, contraception sabotages the body's natural tendencies of fertility. The body is seen as "enemy." It must be controlled. For the sake of her happiness, Jane will stoop to any level to curtail John's dream — she doesn't want all of him — just the part that makes her feel good.

Now, of course, Jane might have some very good reasons for trying to control John. John might be a very poor judge of his own baseball talents, and Jane takes radical measures for his own good, and for "their" own good as a couple. This is where Jane's judgement is pitted against John's. Following through on our analogy, those who practice contraception are saying that the bodies involved are potentially harmful to the couple's mutual pursuit of something good. Nature is trying to tell us fertility is as much a part of sex as baseball is a part of John's personality . . .it is John's perspective that maintains this staunch bond between "John-ness" and "baseball". But then who holds the perspective that fertility is such a good? Who are the contracepting couple pitting themselves against ultimately? Even if both husband and wife are in agreement to the rightness of contraception in their sexual relationship, they are ultimately pitting themselves against the authority of the force that lies behind the natural tendency of the body to procreate. In other words, against the creator of the body and its laws: God.

A contraceptive culture has lead society into an extraordinary physical poverty because the physical aspects of personhood are not held in high esteem. The full needs of the body are crying out to be satisfied but this appeal either falls on deaf ears or is told to be quiet. Perhaps this is possible because certain physical needs are more obvious than others. The need for food, for example, is easier to recognize than the need to live in harmony with the life-giving powers intrinsic to the body. This is why those who disagree so strongly with the immorality of contraception are often so vocal about feeding the poor and reducing population by means of contraception. The American mentality which sees exporting contraceptives as a way of helping other cultures fight poverty fails to appreciate the physical, intellectual, and volitional nature of this perpetual human problem. Instead they choose to do more damage to those who are already suffering.

What is required is a fundamental overhaul of our whole way of thinking about human life and the meaning of human sexuality. If we are talking about abortion, we are talking about babies; if we are talking about babies, we are talking about fertility; if we are talking about fertility, we are talking about the act of procreation; and if we are talking about the act of procreation we are talking about the human body. Like the old song goes, "The leg bone's connected to the hip bone, etc." You can't take a piece out of this puzzle without the whole thing falling in on itself. Contraception slowly destroys and impoverishes the persons involved. It eats away at their respect for life by eating away at their respect for their own bodies and the bodies of others. It swings a balanced view of the human person as a "whole being" into fragments of the truth.

Many young people today clearly have reached a conclusion that the generation before them holds subtly but doesn't admit publicly. Look at the fashions of many youth and the way they treat their bodies: drugs and drinking, body piercing, bizarre hairstyles, body-distorting clothes, excessive sports, muscle enhancing steroids, bulimia and anorexia. The body is attacked and assailed from all sides. It possesses no integrity, no rights, and no dignity.

Who delivered this message to our nation's youth? Who taught them to hold their bodies in contempt?

The apple doesn't fall far from the tree.

Conclusion

On a dreary February day in 1861, Abraham Lincoln stood before a large crowd of his friends and neighbors in Springfield, Illinois. His personal train was about to depart for Washington, D.C. where he would take up the office and responsibilities of president in the nation's darkest hour since it's birth. With deep emotion at this difficult parting, and with typical simplicity and clarity, he chose but a few words to say so much:

> *My friends, no one, not being in my situation can appreciate my feelings of sadness at this parting. To this place, and the kindness of these people, I owe everything. Here I have lived a quarter century, and have passed from a young to an old man. Here my children have been born, and one is buried. I now leave, not knowing when, or whether ever I may return, with a task before me greater than that which rested upon Washington. Without the assistance of that Divine Being, who ever attended him, I cannot succeed. With that assistance I cannot fail . . . let us confidently hope that all will yet be well. To His care commending you, as I hope in your prayers you will commend me, I bid you an affectionate farewell.*[100]

Abraham Lincoln was a religious man in a deep way. True religion is built on the foundation of a sincere relationship to the Divine Being. Human beings are religious by nature, though from time to time, history has presented some cultures, such as atheistic communist Russia, or, sad to say, our increasingly secular American culture, which ignore this religious instinct. Such cultures have collapsed in the past. The Latin roots of the word "religion" mean literally "to bind again." The implication is that something has been undone and needs to be put back together, to

---

100. Donald, *Lincoln*, p. 457

be restored. All the various forms of religious practice are nothing other than manifestations of man's desire to return to God.

Lincoln did not subscribe to a denominational church, and as a young man he found sufficient explanation for life's mysteries in what was called the Doctrine of Necessity, a form of fatalism. As we saw in Chapter One, the young Lincoln, afraid of the power of his own passions, embraced a religion of reason. He went so far as to suggest that this religion be the religion of the people to insure a stable society. As he entered middle age, however, Lincoln turned more and more towards a personal God. The death of his son Willie on February 20, 1862 was a turning point in the religious life of the President. His wife noted that he began at that time to show a real interest in the subject. Donald notes, "He did not experience a religious conversion, though when he looked back on the events of this tragic spring, he recognized that he underwent what he called 'a process of crystallization' in his religious beliefs."[101] He began to read the Bible in earnest and would one day call it "the best gift God has given to man."

But Lincoln's spiritual side had already become evident in his writings and public speeches long before Willie's death. As he grew to understand the moral implications of slavery, his religious faith took greater shape. His disillusionment over the Supreme Court's *Dred Scott* decision and his observations of the calculating and dishonest motivations of certain politicians, with their blatant disregard for justice or the good of the Union – caused him to seek out a higher authority than man's laws and an explanation for the evils men suffer. Donald, so apt a biographer in most instances, fails to appreciate this spiritual evolution in Lincoln, preferring to call it a clever shifting of blame from men to God.[102]

Following the Springfield address, Lincoln continued to evoke the help of God in the short speeches he gave along the way

---

101. Donald, *Lincoln*, p. 337
102. See in particular Donald's explanation of the Second Inaugural Address, pp. 565-568

to Washington, D.C. His first inaugural address prompted the nation to have "a firm reliance on Him, who has never yet forsaken this favored land." Again and again throughout the war he reverted to the idea that behind all the struggles and losses a divine purpose was at work. His religious character, far from being a flimsy sentimentality – something all too often found in the revivalist spirit of his times – was deeply tied to a formed and informed moral conscience which had profited from a life close to nature and suffering. And this, if not enough in itself, was wedded to a heightened sense of the responsibility of leadership before God.

The spirit that Lincoln brought to the presidency was also a humble spirit. Donald again errs in his conclusion that Lincoln's apparent passivity was the result of a fatalistic view of life. True, the president was fond of quoting Hamlet's famous phrase, "There's a divinity that shapes our ends, Rough-hew them how we will." But a man's actions shed light on his words just as in scripture the deeds and words of God are "intrinsically bound up with each other."[103] If we want to understand Abraham Lincoln, we must look at the whole picture. Lincoln's life does not leave us with the impression of a man who threw himself into the changing winds of chance and let the chips fall where they may. On the contrary, he molded and shaped his own destiny, and ultimately the destiny of a nation.

A better explanation for the self-deprecating humor and the continual passing of praise to others was Lincoln's profound humility. Let us correctly define this word. Humility is not self-abasement as an end in itself. Such an understanding flows from the restless marriage of Jansenism and Puritanism. Humility comes

---

103. *Dei Verbum, Dogmatic Constitution on Divine Revelation,* November 18, 1965, found in *Vatican Council II, the Conciliar and Post Conciliar Documents, New Revised Edition 1992,* general editor Austin Flannery, O.P. (Northport, NY: Costello Publishing Company, and Grand Rapids, MI: Wm. B. Eerdmans Publishing Co.)

from a word meaning "earth." It means having your feet on the ground; you are living in reality. The humble man is not moved by flattery – he finds it amusing – not because he has no self-esteem but because flattery overdoes it and he knows the real parameters of his worth. Consequently, he would never sell himself short, either. He knows himself and where he stands in the hierarchy of nature and society.

Humility is closely linked to honesty and fair play. Early on, in his Springfield days, Lincoln often spoke of the need for lawyers to refrain from unfairly charging their clients. Examination of his office records proves he practiced what he preached. For a $600.00 settlement for one client, he charged $3.50. That's about half of one percent. On another occasion, a man in Quincy sent him a check for $25.00 – too exorbitant a fee in Lincoln's estimation for the drawing up of some legal papers. Lincoln wrote back to the man, "You must think I am a high-priced man. You are too liberal with your money. Fifteen dollars is enough for the job." He returned the balance.[104]

Lincoln did not take himself too seriously. He was fond of using his unusual physical appearance as the basis of his humor. He recognized that he came from a world very different from some of his cultured colleagues. On his way home from his first term as Illinois representative, he wrote this thought for an autograph seeker: "I am not a sentimental man; and the best sentiment I can think of is, that if you collect the signatures of all persons who are no less distinguished than I, you will have a very undistinguishing mass of names."[105]

Lincoln was quite mistaken about his lack of distinction. But even after he was elected President he continued to show himself ready to take his accomplishments with a grain of salt: "He had

---

104. Donald, *Lincoln*, p. 148
105. Donald, *Lincoln*, p. 141

been elected President, he said, 'by a mere accident, and not through any merit of mine.' He was 'a mere instrument, an accidental instrument, perhaps I should say,' of the great cause of Union. He called himself 'the humblest of all individuals that have ever been elected to the Presidency,' a man 'without a name, perhaps without a reason why I should have a name.'"[106]

Lincoln showed his humility of heart in other ways. He had that special quality of a leader to accept blame for his subordinate's mistakes. His first Secretary of War, Simon Cameron, was not up to the tremendous challenge of running his department. Stories of mismanagement and botched decisions abounded. He did eventually resign, but the House Committee still kept up their attacks on him. Lincoln spoke up for Cameron. Although he fully approved the proceedings of the committee, he noted that Cameron was not solely responsible for the mistakes. "Not only the President but all the other heads of department were at least equally responsible."[107]

The humility we find in Lincoln grew from the ground of his religious character. He understood that he was subject to a power greater than himself. He expected, along with all mankind, to be called to render account for his life before a throne of perfect justice. The physical height that made it necessary for him to bow in his relations with others was an image of the spiritual height he had reached which kept him in the humble disposition of the publican. God's servants in scripture have always shown this simplicity and the Lord blessed such an attitude when he said, "Those who humble themselves will be exalted, while those who exalt themselves will be humbled."

If Lincoln possessed the strong conviction of his own place before God, he felt even more so the destiny of the United States

---

106. Donald, *Lincoln*, p. 275
107. Donald, *Lincoln*, p. 326

as something watched over, protected, and disciplined by the hand of the Heavenly Father. His understanding of God may have been somewhat abstract, but he did not fail to grasp one of God's essential attributes: justice. In his mind, the integrity of this nation came from its fidelity to the justice that is pleasing to God.

In his Second Inaugural Address, Lincoln made clear his conviction that the nation's sufferings were the direct result of her failure in justice. Justice, in turn, was exacting her fee. Today, these words are engraved on the North wall of the Lincoln Memorial as a reminder of the fundamentally religious character this nation has had up until our present day:

> *On the occasion corresponding to this, four years ago all thoughts were anxiously directed to an impending civil war. All dreaded it, all sought to avert it. While the inaugural address was being delivered from this place, devoted altogether to saving the Union without war, insurgent agents were in the city seeking to destroy it without war, seeking to dissolve the Union and divide effects by negotiation. Both parties deprecated war, but one of them would make war rather than let the nation survive, and the other would accept war rather than let it perish, and the war came.*
>
> *One-eighth of the whole population were colored slaves, not distributed generally over the Union, but localized in the Southern part of it. These slaves constituted a peculiar and powerful interest. All knew that this interest was somehow the cause of the war. To strengthen, perpetuate, and extend this interest was the object for which the insurgents would rend the Union, even by war; while the Government claimed no right to do more than to restrict the territorial enlargement of it. Neither party expected for the war the magnitude or the*

duration which it has already attained. Neither anticipated that the cause of the conflict might cease with, or even before, the conflict itself should cease. Each looked for an easier triumph, and a result less fundamental and astounding. Both read the same Bible and pray to the same God, and each invoked His aid against the other. It may seem strange that any men should dare to ask a just God's assistance in wringing their bread from the sweat of other men's faces, but let us judge not, that we be not judged. The prayers of both could not be answered. That of neither has been answered fully. That Almighty has His own purposes. "Woe unto the world because of offenses; for it must needs be that offenses come, but woe to that man by whom the offense cometh." If we shall suppose that American slavery is one of those offenses which, in the providence of God, must needs come, but which, having continued through His appointed time, He now wills to remove, and that He gives to both North and South this terrible war as the woe due to those by whom the offense came, shall we discern therein any departure from those divine attributes which the believers in a living God always ascribe to Him? Fondly do we hope, fervently do we pray, that this mighty scourge of war may speedily pass away. Yet, if God wills that it continue until all the wealth piled by the bondsman's two hundred and fifty years of unrequited toil shall be sunk, and until every drop of blood drawn with the lash shall be paid by another drawn with the sword, as was said three thousand years ago, so still it must be said "the judgments of the Lord are true and righteous altogether."[108]

---

108. Abraham Lincoln, *The Second Inaugural Address*, March 4, 1865.

These haunting words must send a chill through every American who reads them now in light of Roe v. Wade and the deaths of forty million innocent children since 1973. Even the most elemental religious sense can perceive that no amount of rhetoric, no amount of political posturing, can undo the evil that is and has been done with the sanction of our political leaders. If Lincoln was right, and the country had by divine decree to endure a war so costly to pay for the crime of slavery, what must we conclude lies in store for us in the wake of Roe v. Wade? We pray that Lincoln's words are not prophetic.

I do not intend by this analogy to frighten or depress you. I wish only to place the discussion in its proper context. Whether we like it or not, we are playing with fire. True, abortion does not divide this nation regionally. But geography is only one element of a nation's identity. The next civil war will not mean violence along a specific battle line; it will have the character of a moral eclipse in which the unthinkable has become possible on the most ordinary levels of life. Abortion is already such a thing. In the day that it was legalized, one predicted – against the disclaimers of the pro-abortion party – that euthanasia and assisted suicide would be next on the bill. Has that not come to pass? But even more frightening, is it not true to say that those who possess Judeo-Christian values, who challenge the automatic advance of these evils, have themselves become the threat? Are the lines not drawn, ever more sharply, between those who stand for life and those who stand for an immature sense of liberty at such a high cost? The media at first depicted the pro-lifer as an anachronistic buffoon – the picture has been replaced now by the fanatic psychopath against whom society must arm itself. What is the next step? In a recent description of the kind of people to be feared in our society, former Attorney General Janet Reno listed those who have religious convictions along with those who home school their children.

Some will accuse me of being an alarmist – but I will stand on the historical record. We can either profit from the lessons of the Civil War, or suffer from a youthful arrogance that causes us to throw the teaching of the past behind us like yesterday's newspaper. We must acknowledge that a frightening similarity exists between the debate over abortion and that of slavery. Incredibly similar issues, one of which gave birth to civil war, are again at play. Negotiations over fundamental issues of justice may be slow, but not eternal. In the end, one or the other of the parties involved must triumph. To the victor go the spoils.

Victory means war; and war means leaders. From all we have seen in these pages, a leader is someone whose convictions are informed by truth and fueled by love; who believes that his or her personal morality counts for something in the vast scheme of political life; and who is willing to take into his or her hands the shape of society, even at the risk of death and disgrace. As the Founding Fathers worded it in the Declaration of Independence, fully cognizant of the action they were taking and its probable implications for them personally, " . . . we pledge our lives, our fortunes, and our sacred honor."

Lincoln knew the price of leadership. Even before an assassin's bullet struck him down he had the appearance of a martyr. Who can look without feeling at the photos we have of this great man in the last months of his life? The lines of sleepless nights and dark days etched into his skin. Who in our own time is willing to pay such a price to preserve pure and intact the glory that was promised on that July 4th day in 1776? Who will lay down his life in the service of his country – not in the blare of guns and bombs, nor to the accompaniment of parades and music – but in the slow, cautious, everyday labor of perfecting this great work of human freedom we call the United States of America?

This section opened with the scene of Lincoln's farewell to the people of Springfield. It seemed fitting to end this reflection at the beginning of a presidential journey that would leave for all time such an extraordinary example of leadership and courage. I want, as it were, to place those who presently hold positions in government on that railroad car that bore Lincoln towards Washington. I want them to share with him a sense of urgency for the moral health of this country and take the final step from moderate to leader.

Most importantly, I want to call attention to the one and only source of our strength for what lies ahead. Lincoln was keenly aware that no human power could realize the successful completion of the task he had before him – everything rested solely on the help of God. We, too, must find the light for our path and the sustenance for our souls in the God who defends the cause of the poor. We must become a religious people with a unifying philosophy. We must "bind up the nation's wounds" by being ourselves bound again to our heavenly Father and to the laws he has imprinted on nature and the human heart.

Perhaps this little anecdote sums up by analogy Lincoln's legacy to this country:

When the sculptor Daniel Chester French finished his statue for the Lincoln Memorial, he had a problem. He had hoped that the light from outside would be sufficient to view the massive, seated figure of the President; but the distance from columns to statue and the reality of cloudy Washington weather kept his grand work of marble in the shadows. For six years he wrestled with the problem until he finally reached the conclusion – unusual for statuary – that for the figure to be seen in its true glory, it had to be lit from above.

Biography

Fr. Koys has been a leader in the Right to Life movement for all his priesthood. His philosophical training under some of the best Catholic teachers at The Catholic University of America, in Washington, D.C. and the University of St. Mary the Lake in Mundelein IL provided him with the foundation to see and read the signs of the times in a way that produced a must read book for people of all walks of life. Father took his Master's Degree in Philosophy at C.U.A., and completed his Licentiate in Sacred Theology, at U.S.M.L. both Magna Cum Laude. An organizer of the Chicago chapter of Priest's for Life, he is a requested speaker and promoter of the Pro-life movement. He is presently pastor of Immaculate Conception church in Chicago, IL where he serves a diverse tri-lingual parish. Perhaps, his biggest claim to fame can be summarized in the words (paraphrased) of one high ranking diocesan insider, Fr. Tom, if you keep preaching as you do on abortion, you will make yourself unemployable as a priest in this diocese. Considering the times, Fr. has always consider this to be quite the compliment. This is his inaugural book.

To order additional copies of this book:
Please complete the form below and send to:

CMJ Marian Publishing
P.O. Box 661 • Oak Lawn, IL 60454
toll free 888-636-6799
call 708-636-2995 or fax 708-636-2855
email jwby@aol.com
www.cmjbooks.com

Name _____

Address _____

City _____ State_____ Zip_____

Phone (_____) _____

The Ashes That Still Remain

	QUANTITY	SUBTOTAL
$14.95 x_____ =		$ _____
+ tax (for Illinois residents only) =		$ _____
+ 15% for S & H =		$ _____
TOTAL =		$ _____

Check # _____ Visa   MasterCard   Exp Date ___/___/___

American Express   Discover

Card # _____

Signature _____

211